MICROSOFT

Ajay Sethi is a Delhi-based writer and senior advertising professional. His books include *The Making of the Greatest: Bill Gates* and *The Making of the Greatest: Sony*. He has also written numerous magazine articles and devised several advertising and product promotion campaigns. An MA in English Literature from Delhi University, his interests range from politics and history to philosophy and religion.

Also by the author:

The Making of the Greatest: Bill Gates
The Making of the Greatest: Sony

THE MAKING OF THE GREATEST
MICROSOFT

Ajay Sethi

RUPA

Published by
Rupa Publications India Pvt. Ltd 2021
7/16, Ansari Road, Daryaganj
New Delhi 110002

Sales Centres:
Allahabad Bengaluru Chennai
Hyderabad Jaipur Kathmandu
Kolkata Mumbai

ISBN: 978-93-90918-19-5

First impression 2021

10 9 8 7 6 5 4 3 2 1

The moral right of the author has been asserted.

Printed at Thomson Press India Ltd, Faridabad

CONTENTS

CONTENTS

INTRODUCTION

Not all revolutions lead to upheavals and disruptions in people's lives. There are slow and silent revolutions of the positive kind too. Advancements that seek to introduce new concepts to improve the overall well-being of people, ideas that ensure better ways of doing things and innovations that help to free man from drudgery and labour are surely not short of a revolution. The tech movement that started in the United States in the early 1970s was no doubt one such revolution that would gradually engulf the entire globe and silently invade almost every aspect of our lives. Yes, we're talking about the IT revolution that's changed our lives beyond all measure and recognition. The instant connectivity, the boost to businesses and the push to technology in almost every sphere! Our world has never been the same, and for the better.

What has happened so far is nothing short of a miracle. Of course, a miracle that's been long in the making! It's been a long, drawn-out process involving contributions from different quarters, cross-currents of varied thoughts, research and innovations by some deeply committed individuals. How the whole process has come about, what factors propelled its movement and who were the torchbearers of this process make for a fascinating study, offering, in turn, some deeply enlightening lessons about the working of the human mind and situations.

This work is an attempt to bring you some keen insights into the whole process, with focus on one of its principal actors, a company that was not only a main contributor in the movement but also a pioneer in many ways—Microsoft! A company which was there when it all began, and even after over four decades in the business, continues to call the shots!

A REVOLUTION LIKE NO OTHER

Before we proceed with the story of Microsoft, it would help to study the background and environment in which the company was operating, and the general technological conditions of that time. We know such things don't happen in a day, and no single factor can be construed as the main driver of the process. So, when we look back, we find that as far as the IT revolution is concerned, there have been a number of factors and actors that provided conditions to start and sustain it.

All said and done, in the final analysis, two major factors really worked in its favour. First, by the 1950s, developments in different technologies had been coming to fruition, and their convergence ultimately created the conditions that would allow the IT revolution to happen and to produce better and smarter devices. Second were the geographical and physical advantages the US offered, which served ideal conditions for the beginning of the process.

Becoming the Overriding Technology

Once the process began, it became virtually unstoppable. As advancements in the technology started to happen, increasing uses of IT could be found across the board in other disciplines—so much so that in time, it has emerged as the 'mother of all technologies', making major contributions to improve the efficiency of other disciplines.

In the beginning, as the name suggests, the computer was a calculating device. In fact, manual and mechanical computing devices have existed since ancient times. From the Abacus in about 2300 BC, there had been some progress towards mechanical analogue computers in the medieval Islamic world in the eleventh and twelfth centuries. By 1912, with the advent of electricity in the early twentieth century, Arthur Pollen, a leading British journalist and businessman, was able to produce one of the world's first electrically-powered analogue computers, patented as the Argo clock.

Given its utility, advancements in the field had been taking place, with IBM (International Business Machines Corporation) supplying analogue computers to assist in the building of the first atom bomb, and later the University of Pennsylvania developing the first electronic computer, ENIAC (Electronic Numerical Integrator and Computer), which was formally dedicated to the US on 15 February 1946. It was initially produced for calculating artillery firing tables. It was a high point in a long quest. Researchers had been essentially concerned about improving the efficiency of the computer by harnessing the power of electricity. Initially, this was done by developing transistors and, later, integrating a large number of transistors on a single chip, first using germanium and then silicon. It was the integrated circuit (IC) that led to the development of the microprocessor. It was this development that changed the electronics landscape of the world and subsequently of all the other technologies. Further advancements made it possible to produce chips on a mass scale, which meant lowering of cost. It also helped to make new computers and devices lighter, more compact and easier to handle. At the time, people didn't know where all this might lead, but gradually, the computer revolution would come to have a positive effect on almost all fields of human activity — from automobile to aviation, agriculture to education, medicine and nuclear physics to space sciences and printing and publishing. Computerized devices could be found everywhere, ranging from people's homes to high-end nuclear facilities. The revolution was on.

However, there have been some other physical factors too that enabled this revolution: first, the contribution of the US as a physical and technical entity, and second, the convergence of different technologies towards furthering this process.

America and Americanism

Although the US can't boast of much history, yet interestingly, the modern history of humanity is very closely intertwined with that of America, its growth and development. If we draw a line at the year 1500, we find the discovery of the 'new world' to be crucial in shaping up many major events and developments of the modern times. It spurred trade across the globe to an unprecedented level which in turn boosted innovation and produced new inventions. The Americas, and especially the US, provided safe havens for persecuted religious and disadvantaged groups, besides offering wide, open, virgin lands for setting up facilities for entrepreneurs to experiment and grow. Following this, the US emerged as a leader in economic growth—the land of opportunity offering a range of advantages to an individual seeking self-actualization.

'Heaven and earth never agreed better to frame a place for man's habitation,' said John Smith, the British explorer who played a leading role in setting up the first permanent English settlement at Jamestown, Virginia, in the early seventeenth century. The US is about three times the size of India, and most of it comprises good, arable and inhabitable land. This was always a major asset for the country. In addition to this, the discovery of oil in the nineteenth century, coupled with other natural resources, made it a powerful and rich nation in the long run. But no amount of resources can make a country rich and powerful until they're managed well— and that's where the US succeeded in scoring over most of the other nations. Any community or society moves on the basis of ideas, its core faith and beliefs. In fact, it was the churning after the 1500s that put the West on a different footing than the East and threw up radical new ideas about socio-economic reforms and management and the individual's role in society. Many earlier developments had been leading up to this point, and after the invention of mechanical metal movable-type printing in the mid-fifteenth century, which spurred the spread of knowledge, these came to fruition.

In earlier societies, especially till the sixteenth century, the community had had a more or less complete stranglehold over the individual's liberty and the choices he made. In Christian countries, it exercised power through the Church and a variety of other political institutions. If the individual needed divine help for anything, he had to go through the church, the de facto 'divine office' of God on Earth. But then, as the ecclesiastics started to become corrupt and authoritarian, there was a reaction to such practices, and Protestantism was born. The Reformists renounced the authority of the Catholic Church and the Pope, and gave the scriptures, the Bible (the 'Word' of God), the status of the supreme authority, above the priests. Although the church didn't disappear in the Protestant world, the new philosophy and ideas gave the individual greater leeway in matters of religion. The individual could attain salvation by 'faith alone' by 'dealing with God' through the scriptures and the Bible. The Church was no longer the sole authority whose sanctions were needed for individual actions. In a way, these basic precepts freed the individual from the authority of the Church to a large extent. Some writers have thus called Martin Luther, the leader of the movement, the 'patron saint of individualism'. And if we look closely, Protestantism and individualism are inextricably linked — in fact, they are two faces of the same coin. Later, a whole array of new ideas — individual liberty, freedom and democracy — flowed from these basic precepts.

To begin with, what helped Protestantism was the invention of the printing press in the fifteenth century and spread of new ideas thereon. Once the reaction started, it virtually opened up a Pandora's box. A variety of different strands of beliefs started making their appearance. The first one to kindle the dormant feelings was Martin Luther (1483–1546), a German professor and a monk. Another prominent figure was John Calvin (1509–1564), a French pastor, originally a humanist lawyer. Once the fire had been lit, it became a kind of people's movement, with religious scholars and intellectuals of all hues and shades across Europe jumping into the fray. John Knox, a Scottish theologian;

Henry VIII, the king of England; Thomas Cranmer, the Archbishop of Canterbury (1489–1556); Philipp Melanchthon, a German theologian; Thomas Muntzer, a German preacher; Martin Bucer, a German ecclesiastic, and Huldrych Zwingli, a Swiss scholar were some of the key sixteenth-century figures who were involved in the movement and played an important role in bringing about the change. Resentment against the established Catholic Church had run so deep among people that it swept all of Europe, and more and more people began to break off from the old tradition. The counter-reaction by the Catholic Church was to excommunicate and persecute the leaders of the Reformation, as the movement had come to be called. Its appeal and spread can be gauged by the fact that as of 2021, there are 800 million to one billion Protestants in the world, in a total of 2.5 billion Christians, accounting for about one third of the overall number.

The discovery of the Americas too helped the movement, as the new world offered a safe haven for those persecuted in Europe. Starting from the seventeenth century, there was a great influx in the new continent from Europe to different regions of North and South America, where the Europeans established new colonies. In all this, the US emerged as a major attraction because of the many advantages it offered. Apart from its natural resources and other geographical advantages, the US, with its established social and political systems inherited from the parent country, seemed more attractive to the immigrants. In present day too, the US has the largest population among all the American countries.

These facts offer us useful insights into how the US emerged as an engine of growth in the modern times, not only for the West but for the entire world. True, it did possess many natural geographical advantages, but what helped it to really move ahead were its progressive political and social ideas, and above all the Protestant-individualistic spirit. Although there has been some disagreement among scholars about the connection between capitalism (propelled by individualism) and the Reformation, most historians agree that Protestantism played a key role in the rise of capitalism. Max Weber, a major sociologist of the early twentieth century, found a direct link between capitalism and Protestantism. In his work, *The Protestant Ethic and the Spirit of Capitalism*, he argued that the new spirit of individualism that laid emphasis on work ethic led to the development of capitalism. Unshackled from the constraints of overbearing authority, the individual could pursue his goals and find fulfillment the way he desired.

According to Weber, societies that had more Protestants also had had a greater capitalist growth. He called such individuals 'heroic entrepreneurs'. Another point that needs to be emphasized here is that Calvin believed that some people were God's 'chosen ones', while others were damned. This belief prompted people to work hard and find the signs of being the 'chosen ones' in their success and status symbols. The richer you are, the more entitled to God's grace!

Given these factors, the pursuit of success and the spirit of competition have, in many ways, defined the various societal trends in the US and have been the running themes in most of its major literary works. America has been called the land of opportunity, and writers and poets have passionately talked of the great 'American Dream'. In *The Great Gatsby* by F. Scott Fitzgerald, the hero's single-minded pursuit of the attainment of wealth and status forms the crux of the story. Referring to his love interest Daisy Buchanan, the protagonist Jay Gatsby says, 'Her voice is full of money.'

Canadian-American writer Saul Bellow constantly talks of the country's greatness and its preoccupation with success. The main character Von Humboldt Fleisher in *Humboldt's Gift* describes his own state as, 'I have vertigo from success.' Talking of the magnitude of America's operation, Bellow says that America was 'God's experiment.' 'The USA was a big operation, very big. The more it, the less we.' Arthur Miller's *Death of a Salesman*, a standard textbook in American schools, also grapples with the ideas of success and failure. Its protagonist, the 63-year-old New York salesman Willy Loman epitomizes the values that the society cherishes and upholds in a rather tragic way. Ayn Rand, a Russian Jew who had migrated to the US in 1926, found in America the liberty she had been yearning for. Her novels *The Fountainhead* and *Atlas Shrugged* became bestsellers in the 1940s and '50s. A great votary of individual's rights, she insisted on man's right to his own life, liberty and pursuit of happiness. She believed that man has the 'right to exist for his own sake, neither sacrificing himself to others, nor sacrificing others to himself.'

Convergence of Technologies

After the invention of the wheel, mankind had embarked on a new road to progress. Subsequently, the discovery and use of different metals somewhat hastened this process. Gold and silver were predominantly of aesthetic value but copper, being soft and malleable, was helpful in making utensils and other articles. Later with the discovery of tin and zinc, the hardened copper alloys of bronze and brass could be made which provided greater variety in utility items. Although discovered earlier, it was the increasing use of iron after 1200 BC that really transformed the human situation. The Iron Age, as it came to be called, set humanity on a new trajectory of growth. By the beginning of the Christian era (AD 1), humanity had started to build new civilizations, quite 'modern' by the standards of those days. However, man still had a long distance to travel.

The convergence of the technologies had begun from the earliest days. The process was like laying building blocks on one another to move up. But then the real 'modern era' was inaugurated after 1500 — after the invention of the printing press that helped to spread knowledge. The discovery of the Americas, the

Reformation and the Industrial Revolution of Europe after the seventeenth century continued to aid this process. Yet, what the progress lacked was a supply of wholesale energy as the mechanical devices, however sophisticated, were not able to free man from the drudgery of labour.

All these events were leading up to the world we see today. By the middle of the nineteenth century, much progress had been made in almost all spheres, with the invention of a variety of mechanical devices. Humanity was waiting for sources that could ensure mass energy supply to drive machines in large numbers. The commercial exploitation of petroleum in the mid-nineteenth century and the invention of electricity proved to be major steps in this direction. Electricity was a wonder invention that would be used to power all kinds of devices, and give a major thrust to human progress. Michael Faraday (1791–1867), who's regarded as the 'father of electricity', and later Thomas Alva Edison (1847–1931) and Nikola Tesla (1856–1943) contributed to its invention and development in a significant way. By the end of the 1880s, small electric stations had started coming up in different US cities. First the discovery of oil and then electricity had set humanity on the fast track of growth.

To understand how we've reached the computer of present times, we need to be aware of two different streams of technology developments: one in electricity and electronics, moving from vacuum tubes to transistors and ICs; and the other in specific fields, moving from black-and-white photography to colour, from tape recorders to CDs and pen drives, and from telexes and teleprinters to fax and email. These developments were taking place independent of each other and without much reference to one another. However, since the subject being discussed here is the computer, and in particular Microsoft, we will be studying how the growth in electronics led to its development. Separate research was being undertaken in other areas too, leading to more sophisticated devices. All these later merged to produce the smart devices we have today. With regard to computers, with every passing year, the chip manufacturers have continued to make their microprocessors faster and more powerful. The difference between the earlier and later versions is primarily the speed—advanced microprocessors can perform millions of tasks per second and quickly move data between various memory locations. Thus, the stage was set for phenomenal growth in the computer industry, leading up to all kinds of increasingly efficient and smarter computers and servers.

Parallel to this, other technologies too had been undergoing advancements. And with convergence of technologies being an inevitable process, new smarter devices would begin to appear much to the delight of the consumer. If we look at today's computer, its monitor has come from the TV, keyboard from the typewriter, visual displays from earlier cameras and developments in cinematography, etc. '(In future) people will carry around small devices that allow them to constantly stay in touch and do electronic business from wherever they are. They will be able to check the news, see flights they have booked, get information from financial markets, and do just about anything else on these devices,' Bill Gates wrote in his 1999 book *Business@ the Speed of Thought*.[1] All that has come true, and yet we can say, 'You ain't seen nothin' yet!'

CHANGING FACE OF COMPUTER

Truly, the advancements of the 1950s and '60s, especially the developments in the field of microprocessor technology, had put the computer industry on a different trajectory. Still, nobody knew how things would play out in the future—and the way they did astonished even its most enthusiastic proponents.

So, before we go into the details, it's essential to have an overview of the growth in microprocessor technology.

Microprocessor—The Game Changer

The earlier radio was a big bulky device that would occupy the whole table. Its big size was essentially on account of the large vacuum tubes that performed the function of controlling and relaying the electrical current. These tubes had existed since the beginning of the century and were used in practically all the electrical devices. Subsequent research in the field to improve these devices led to the invention of the transistor in 1947 — a major step forward. However, what totally changed the electronics landscape was the integration of a large number of transistors on a small, flat metal piece (first germanium and later silicon), and was called integrated circuit, ASIC or simply IC. In 1949, Werner Jacobi, a scientist working in Siemens, had filed for a patent for an early version of the IC that had only five transistors. It was a nascent idea that couldn't be fully implemented. More serious attempts with substantial advancements were made in the late fifties with scientists like Jack Kilby, Robert Noyce, Kurt Lehovec, Jean Hoerni and some others.

However, as there were conflicting claims as to who actually invented the IC, a patent war ensued, with the American press finally narrowing down the list to Jack Kilby and Robert Noyce. Kilby was later awarded the Nobel Prize in Physics in 2000 for his 'part in the invention of the integrated circuit.' The IC paved the way for the development of the microprocessor that is the heart—the controlling unit—of a computer or machine. An IC forms the basis of a microprocessor that may contain more than one IC.

As we've indicated earlier, with the passage of time, the convergence of technologies had continued to bring us more advanced and sophisticated products. So, when the scientists were able to integrate a large number of transistors on a single chip, it was considered a major breakthrough, but few had realized the enormous possibilities it was about to open up for mankind. Another major impact of these developments was that gradually it became possible to produce chips on a mass scale, which meant lowering of cost. The increasing power of the microprocessor, and consequently its mass production, were set to change the entire landscape of technology and, in turn, the future of mankind. In time, microprocessor-backed technology would impact every field of human activity.

An overview of the progress of the microprocessor gives us an idea about its increased power and capability over time. While Intel's first-generation microprocessor, the 4004, had 2,300 transistors, there were later improved versions such as the 8080 in 1974 with 6,000 transistors, the 8085 in 1976 with 6,500 transistors, and so on. The Intel Pentium IV released in 2000 contained 42 million transistors. In a March 2017 spectrum.ieee.org report, Rachel Courtland quoted Kaizad Mistry of Intel as claiming that the company could pack more than 100 million transistors in each square millimeter of a chip.[2]

Thus, with every passing year, companies have continued to make faster and more powerful microprocessors. The difference between the earlier and later versions is mainly the speed — the advanced microprocessors can perform millions of tasks per second and quickly move data between various memory locations. The computer industry was ready to bring the PC (personal computer) into the homes of millions of users. It was also time for real talent to seize the opportunity.

Computer Comes out of The Lab

The decade beginning with 1970 could be considered the starting point of the advent of the small computer — microcomputer or personal computer. The earlier advancements, especially the designing of the microprocessor, had fired the imagination of all kinds of computer scientists and engineers who envisaged building new devices over a variety of microprocessors. It was a golden opportunity for new entrepreneurs to set up shop and move the process forward. And this is precisely what happened starting in the late 1960s and early '70s. It was as if the new developments had extended an open invitation to all those with talent and imagination, grit and gumption! In other words, the basic foundations of the industry were being laid during this time. This could also be called the period of consolidation. With every passing day, the general climate had begun to improve, and this helped to encourage and enthuse the people involved in the process. In both hardware and software fields, major advances had begun to take place.

On the one hand, many young entrepreneurs with little previous experience but who were passionate and driven, like Bill Gates, Paul Allen, Steve Jobs, Steve Wozniak, Michael Dell and others, had ventured out into the field. On the other, industry veterans like Gordon Moore and Robert Noyce of Intel, and Sandy Lerner and Leonard Bosack of Cisco were setting up their companies. Intel was established by semiconductor pioneers Moore and Noyce in 1968, AMD (Advanced Micro Devices) by Walter Jeremiah Sanders and seven others in 1969, SAP by five former IBM employees in 1972, Microsoft by Bill Gates and Paul Allen in 1975, Apple Inc. by Steve Wozniak and Steve Jobs in 1976 and Oracle Corporation by Larry Ellison, Bob Miner and Ed Oates in 1977. The year 1982 saw the setting up of Adobe Inc. by John Warnock and Charles Geschke; Sun Microsystems Inc. by Vinod Khosla, Scott McNealy, Andy Bechtolsheim and Bill Joy and Compaq Computer Corporation by Rod Canion, Jim Harris and Bill Murto. Dell Inc. and Cisco Systems, Inc. were started in 1984 by Michael Dell, and Sandy Lerner and Leonard Bosack, respectively, and Corel Corporation in the following year by Michael Cowpland. IBM, which was originally established as CTR (Computing-Tabulating-Recording Company) in 1911 was later renamed IBM in 1924. Then there is Hewlett-Packard that was originally founded by Bill Hewlett and David Packard in 1939, and split in 2015, with HP Inc. operating the PC and printer business.

Making Computer a Household Item

Or, in other words, giving it mass appeal!

Yes, the companies had been established. But for a company to survive, it needs a revenue growth, which could only come from volume production and sales increase. The obvious question was, why would a common person buy an expensive electronic device unless it gave him value for money (for instance, Apple II, delivered in April 1977, was priced at $1,295)? This problem could only be addressed by making the product more useful for people at large.

To begin with, a home computer was a sophisticated calculator, an information-storing machine and a gaming device, all rolled into one. It essentially appealed to the hobbyists and gaming enthusiasts. However, to boost the sales, one needed to push the envelope. To widen the base there was a need to heighten the personal computer's utility value. Some got thinking that as it was a 'logic' machine, it should ideally be able to do anything—write letters and articles, design cars and planes or alter photos and videos. And thus, people got working to produce applications to popularize it. We need to clarify here that work on a variety of such applications had been happening all along, but with advancements in microprocessor technology, the imagination got wings.

'The home computer that's ready to work, play and grow with you,' read one of the early ads of Apple II. Another one with a headline, 'How to buy a personal computer,' talked of how thousands of people, including 'businessmen, students and hobbyists had already discovered the Apple computer' and had been using it for 'financial management, complex problem solving or just plain fun.' So if the man of the house could track his share investments, keep accounts or records with its help, the lady could manage her domestic expenses better and children could have fun with their favourite cartoon characters or learn how their car runs.

The first 'trinity' of personal computers was the Commodore PET 2001 by Commodore International, Apple II by Apple Inc. and TRS-80 by Tandy Corporation, which were launched in 1977. Among this 'trinity', Apple II got a head start as it was able to present VisiCalc (Visible Calculator, the accounting software, precursor to Lotus 1-2-3 and Microsoft's Excel), along with other applications. It widened the computer's scope and helped to re-position the home computer as a business-application device also. Yet much ground needed to be covered.

Beginning in the 1980s and all through the '90s much work was done to popularize the concept of home (personal) computer and make it more useful for the general households. The general areas identified for the purpose, to begin with, were word processing, accounting, presentations and photo editing/ management and designing, as these directly concerned general people and also professionals.

One of the first focus areas in this respect was word processing, as it was a regular task people engaged in. Editing, copying, cutting and pasting, storing of the texts, etc., would take much labour out of the process. As a result, in the early eighties, many computer engineers and scientists made a foray into the area of word processing. Among the more successful ones around this time was WordStar, which offered automatic mail merging and controlled 25 per cent of the market. In time, it found stiff competition, first from WordPerfect, owned by Corel, and later from Microsoft Word. In the late 1980s and early '90s, WordPerfect had become the dominant word processing software because of its many plus points like macro capabilities, 'reveal codes' features and high-quality support. But gradually, it began to lose ground to Microsoft Word, first, because it was late in releasing its Windows version, and second, on account of Microsoft offering Word bundled with Microsoft Office. WordPerfect was first sold to Novell, and then to Corel in 1996. In the meantime, Microsoft Word had stolen a march on it to become the industry standard. WordPerfect has very little market share at present, only enjoying some support within the legal fraternity.

Accounting software was another major gift of this time. The software's usefulness was without question, and the smarter it was, the easier it would make work for the harried accountant. Developers were working overtime to outdo one another in producing effective software. In this respect, some initial work had been done in the early sixties by Richard Mattessich, a business economist and emeritus professor at the University of British Columbia. Later the development of LANPAR (LANguage for Programming Arrays at Random) by Rene K. Pardo and Remy Landau in 1970 put it on a different footing. Further, VisiCalc developed by Bob Frankston and Dan Bricklin of Software Arts and offered with Apple II in 1977, was another major advancement in the field. New competitors that emerged on the scene were Super Calc, Multiplan and later Lotus 1-2-3. SuperCalc, which was next in the line, was an improvement on VisiCalc and entered the market subsequently. As it scored over VisiCalc, it got ahead in the market. A year later, Microsoft introduced its Multiplan that was a step ahead and was targeted towards systems running CP/M, MS-DOS, Xenix and many other operating systems.

Subsequently, the competition narrowed down to Multiplan and Lotus 1-2-3 developed by Lotus Software in 1983 for IBM. In time, Lotus became so popular that people would ask for the 'Lotus Computer'. According to Bill Gates, the main reason for Multiplan lagging behind was that they had tried to align it with too many ports. While Microsoft was working on improving Multiplan, Lotus began to run into rough weather because of some technical issues. Microsoft released an improved version of Multiplan, called Excel, in 1985 for Apple Macintosh, which for the first time had a graphical interface. In 1987, Excel 2.0 was released with Windows. As Excel was now part of Windows, which was a preferred O/S (operating system), its popularity soared. Lotus began to lose ground, giving way to Excel which eventually became the dominant spreadsheet.

Presentation software was another area of focus during this time. For large, modern business houses, 'presentations' were becoming necessary, and the existing tools were expensive and cumbersome. Companies such as Trollman, Genigraphics (division of General Electric), Dicomed and others had graduated from the simple slide projections to computer workstations on which presentations graphics software could run a large number of slides. But these devices still had their downsides. An exponential growth in the PC market again gave a fillip to activity in this area, with many industry players entering the fray to develop smart presentation software. Interestingly, as in the case of the word processing and accounting software, here too Microsoft was able to steal a march over its competitors ultimately. Since the three applications have remained its major products and revenue earners, their growth and evolution have been dealt with in a comprehensive manner in the chapter 'Windows and Office—Star Performers'.

Some other areas in which new activities had spurred developments were those related to visual media and designing. Given the power of new microprocessors, a variety of software could be developed to edit or alter pictures, create new graphics and produce industrial designs. Adobe Inc., established in 1982, and Corel Corporation founded, in 1985, took a lead in this respect and opened up new vistas for designers and illustrators. Photoshop, the main software developed by Adobe, has, in fact, over the years become a verb, a generic term today—e.g., 'this image has been photoshopped'. It's a graphic software that's become an industry standard and is used today for a variety of graphics-editing and digital-art jobs. While Photoshop is used for 'raster' (rectangular form) graphic editing, the CorelDRAW developed by Corel Corporation is a 'vector' (2D) graphic editor extensively used for designing, modifying and editing images and page layouts.

If book layout designing was here, then could car designing be far behind? Designing software have also proved to be a boon for industrial designing—whether it's for a car, airplane or any other utility item. Industrial designing and special effects software came into their own with the setting up of Autodesk, Inc. by John Walker and Dan Drake in 1982, while the former is also the co-author of AutoCAD, one of the leading software in this field. Their software continues to be used for a variety of applications in architecture, civil and structural designing and also in 3D animation in film visual effects.

That's the story till the early 1990s, which incidentally continues till this date. The next shift came about with the advent of the Internet, which could even be termed the second wave. Even earlier engineers had been able to align one computer to another by establishing LANs (local area networks) within limited spaces. As efforts were being made to create the Internet ('network of networks') to connect different computers located at a distance (worldwide vs. local), the breakthrough was achieved with the creation of the World Wide Web in 1989 by British scientist Tim Berners-Lee, while conducting research at CERN, Switzerland. He was able to link different computers that could be accessible from any node. He wrote the web browser in 1990, which was released outside CERN in 1991. With further developments in the 1990s, an entire new world opened up before people—electronic messaging, voice mail, video interface, Internet calling, e-tailing—like never before. If the railways and aviation have been the earlier major connectors for humanity, the Internet has proved to be the next big thing.

This process spawned a whole new trend of new IT activities, which necessitated the development of new applications and software. The world's choices had widened from email to e-tailing, from image transmission to video streaming, from data storage to big data and from data sharing to cloud computing. This connectivity has also led to the creation of many social media tools. Besides the general media of newspapers and TV, people have also been able to connect with each other through social media, with applications like Facebook, WhatsApp, Instagram, Twitter, etc., playing an important role in their lives.

Another major positive outcome of computer development has been enterprise management. Its role in improving efficiency and resource management of companies has been mind boggling. Today, no medium- or large-sized operation can afford to go without comprehensive computerization of its operation. Whether it's a car factory or an airplane manufacturing facility, hospital or hotel, bank or insurance operation, computerization is the way to go. And over time it has grown into a multi-billion-dollar business worldwide, with almost every second computer company engaged in it.

Literally, too, the computer's face has been changing. Mainframes have always been in a class of their own, but since the advent of home computers, the overall design of the device has been evolving and changing, from the earlier TV-supported and hardware-heavy machines to sleeker and more compact ones. From the Apple I and II to the smart iPhone of present day, we've come a long way with the options of tablets, touch-screen models and foldable laptops also available.

GATES AND ALLEN—SEIZING THE OPPORTUNITY

gainst this backdrop, Microsoft's story is both interesting and enlightening. Even after over 40 years of existence, it has remained one of the few tech companies with sufficient resilience and resolve, to not only survive but thrive in a fiercely competitive environment. It began when the revolution had started and continues to rule the waves with an impressive performance. It's one of the very few companies in the world to have crossed the market capitalization of over a trillion dollars, and has an annual turnover that puts it among the top tech companies in the world. As of fiscal year 2019–2020, it recorded a revenue of $143 billion with a net income of $44.3 billion. In comparison to its peers, it's ahead of IBM ($73.6 billion in revenue with a net income of $5.53 billion in 2020), though behind Apple ($274.51 billion in revenue with a net income of $57.41 billion in 2020). Its other close competitors, Alphabet (parent company of Google) had revenue of $182.53 billion and net income of $40.27 billion in 2020 and Amazon was at $386.06 billion in revenue with a net income of $21.33 billion in 2020.

The journey of Microsoft up to this point has been exciting and thrilling for those involved and full of challenges. It also makes a fascinating read. In other words, it is also the story of Gates and Allen to begin with, which in time expanded to encompass a vast domain, in fact, the world. To understand it in a comprehensive manner, it is essential to first focus on the founders.

Bill Gates—The Early Years

Bill Gates was born on 28 October 1955, in Seattle, Washington, in an upper middle-class family. His father, William H. Gates Sr., was a prominent lawyer and his mother was a teacher and community activist. Gates is the second child in the family, with two sisters Kristianne (Kristi), one year older, and younger sister,

Libby. The Gates were important members of the local Protestant community and enthusiastically participated in community affairs. Gates's mother had quit her teaching job earlier, devoting her time mainly to looking after her family.

By all accounts, it was a happy, loving family, devoted to Christian values, and the members were caring and supportive of one another. The children liked to play indoor board games together like Risk and Monopoly. Gates especially enjoyed non-team events liked roller skating, and as he grew up, tennis and water skiing. Owing to their Protestant background, the family encouraged competition—a trait that would stay with Gates for the rest of his life. Given its history and immigration pattern, the US has been generally driven by the Protestant spirit, and it has often been argued by thinkers and sociologists that behind the success of capitalism and the US emerging as an engine of growth for the world is its Protestant spirit and stress on individualism. The Gates family, imbued with this spirit, encouraged competition among the new generation, and continued to instill positive and practical values that got ingrained in children at an early age. 'It didn't matter whether it was hearts or pickle ball or swimming to the dock... There was always a reward for winning, and there was always a penalty for losing,' a visitor to the family once noted.[3]

Bill Gates was a rather shy and quiet child. Somewhat withdrawn, he would keep to himself and wouldn't freely mix around with other kids at school. He slowly began to withdraw into his shell, becoming introverted and aloof. He would be easily bored, and when bored, he would need some change. At home, he would rebel against his mother's discipline and at school, would often get into trouble with other children and even talk back to his teachers. Sometimes, just to check, when his father would call and ask, 'What are you doing?', his reply would be, 'Thinking. Don't you ever think?' His parents had started to get worried and feared he might land up as a loner. They even consulted a counsellor who advised them to let him be. In his opinion, things would change with time.

They thus sought to channelize his energies in positive, productive directions. They made him participate in boy scouting activities (he even earned his Eagle Scout badge) and also encouraged him to take part in team sports. They were happy to discover his growing interest in reading and so fuelled his curiosity further through science fiction books. These steps worked to improve matters and things began to change. Although his parents were supportive of the public education system, they decided to put him in the upscale Lakeside School in Seattle. They thought the new school would challenge him and address their concerns. And to their pleasant surprise, it was this new school that turned out to be the 'change' they were seeking.

The Mothers' Club of the school had used proceeds from a school's rummage sale to buy a teletype terminal on time-sharing basis for students to have a greater familiarity with the computer. After over two decades of its growth in the late sixties, the computer had begun to come out of the elite laboratories and high-end space centres. It was now seen in schools and university laboratories. 'Fascination of the new' is usually a characteristic associated with young people. The older generation, with an attitude of 'Been there done that!', tends to be blasé. We can say it was this phenomenon coupled with the typical 'youth enthusiasm' that was the germinating seed of Microsoft. Gates, who was an intelligent child and good at math, was quite taken in with the machine. While in the previous school he would often feel quite bored, here, he had found an object of interest. Besides this, he also found a 'fellow traveller', Paul Allen, who was about three years older than him and was equally passionate about computers. Gates later wrote that it was difficult for him to stay away from the machine. 'There's something neat about the machine,' he said. 'It was hard to tear myself away from a machine at which I could so unambiguously demonstrate success.'

Two Young Geeks with Dreams in Their Eyes

The duo had found their calling in life, and also a common purpose. Gates was grateful to Allen for keeping him by his side. 'Kids those days didn't usually hang out with younger kids,' he recalls. Both had formed a kind of camaraderie. During the day, they would be busy in the computer room of their school and later at the Washington University library. As Allen's parents were librarians, the kids had access to the facility and would often land up there in the evening to hone their computer skills. They would be forever busy in the computer room, tinkering with the machine and experimenting with it—so much so that they even launched onto making new programmes and devising methods to hack the computer. When their time on the computer had been exhausted, Gates and his friends exploited the weaknesses in the system to obtain more time. For this, they were punished by the school authorities and banned from using the computer for some time. Later, when Gates was asked to write the information system of the school for scheduling of students in classes, he put himself in a class with a 'disproportionate number of girls' by manipulating the programme.

However, on the positive side, he was able to write a programme that allowed the user to play tic-tac-toe (noughts and crosses) against the computer. Along with Paul Allen, he formed a business arrangement Traf-O-Data, which obtained basic data from traffic counters and created reports to facilitate traffic engineers to regulate the traffic better. Gates also undertook a programming assignment at a power plant, as both his school headmaster and parents thought that some exposure to professional, practical life would do him good.

Allen recalls that he would often dress up in sports coat and tie, with leather briefcase and all, and bus it down to the local computer gurus' offices in search of discarded code. While code would be easily available to employees of the companies, Allen and Gates had to hunt for it. Allen would boost the smaller Gates into dumpsters and they would get 'these coffee-stained texts (of computer code) from behind the offices'. Once they found a printout of an important source code that unlocked a lot of secrets. Although Bill Gates and Paul Allen were basically different people, they still had a lot in common. Both were science inclined, good at math and shared a common passion for this new wonder machine and, above all, had a sincerity of purpose and sense of loyalty to each other. Such was the groundwork being laid by destiny for both of them to subsequently collaborate and form Microsoft.

As Allen was senior to Gates, he left Lakeside School earlier and went on to join the Washington University. Bill Gates graduated from the school in 1973, with an impressive 1590 out of 1600 in SAT (Scholastic Aptitude Test), and was able to secure admission to Harvard. 'My mother was filled with pride the day I was admitted here,' Gates recalled in his 2007 Harvard commencement address. Although Gates had opted for Law as a major since the family was more inclined towards this profession, he had also signed for other science subjects.

Despite clear options on the paper, Gates would spend more time in the computer facilities than other classes—such was the pull of computer. Although Bill Gates and Paul Allen had parted ways after school, they had kept in touch. As the computer bug had bitten the two badly, they wished to continue with their earlier pursuits. Over time, Gates was able to persuade Allen to relocate to Boston, so that the two could continue with their programming ventures. Allen secured a job with Honeywell in Boston, and the two formed an informal arrangement to pick up programming assignments as and when they could. Gates recalls those days of struggle and how they were not deterred by rejections. They would call big companies for assignments, and the reply would be, 'You kids are just high school guys. We do this work ourselves.'

Around this time, computer-related activity had begun to pick up pace in the US, especially on the West Coast. Gates and Allen had been waiting for something major to materialize to give a push to their dreams. An old saying 'Fortune favours the brave,' is surely applicable in their case. As luck would have it, Allen was crossing the Harvard Yard one chilly morning when he spotted the January 1975 edition of a magazine,

Popular Electronics, at a stall. What it had on the cover immediately caught Allen's eye. It had the picture of the Altair 8800 kit, a new microcomputer, on the cover, with the description: 'Project Breakthrough! World's First Minicomputer Kit to Rival Commercial Models... "Altair 8800". Save over $1,000.' Initially the concept of the 'kit' was to encourage people, especially hobbyists, to assemble their own machine and save on cost.

We need to remind ourselves that at this stage, the microcomputer (or later what IBM called the personal computer), hadn't yet entered general households. Around this time, at best, it was a gaming device or a gadget for hobbyists. The new Altair 8800, manufactured by MITS (Micro Instrumentation and Telemetry Systems), was not a finished product. It was just a rectangular box with several rows of tiny toggle switches across the front. With no software, disk drive or keyboard, the buyer had to assemble it from a kit. Unlike the modern PC that has upwards of millions of bytes of RAM (Random Access Memory), it had just 256 bytes. It also offered an opportunity to programming enthusiasts to develop software for it. Allen saw in it the opportunity they had been waiting for. He grabbed the magazine and ran to Gates and suggested that they develop the programme for it. It was not the first microcomputer, but the first to catch people's imagination. Given computer prices in those days, it was economically priced, and as a result, had begun to become popular with computer enthusiasts. Producing software for this machine could bring them the head start they had been looking for. Allen was quite enthusiastic about it and kept telling Gates, 'Let's do it. Let's start a company.'

When they contacted the company, the founder Ed Roberts told them, 'We are getting about 10 letters a day from people.' 'I'd tell them whoever writes it first, gets the job.' After they got the go-ahead on the project their next challenge was how and where to write the programme. The first hurdle was that they didn't have the machine, and didn't want to spend on it just for the purpose. However, both did have access to computers, Gates at the University and Allen at his company. As they both sensed in it their big opportunity, they decided to have a go at it with all their mind and heart. Unmindful of rest or sleep, or even food, Gates got down to it at a furious pace. Occasionally, he would grab a bite here or there and curl up in a corner for rest; he would even dose off at the keyboard. As Allen was at Honeywell nearby; he would come regularly to assist and contribute his bit. While Allen worked on the simulator, Gates worked on the interpreter. They even hired some other Harvard students to assist them in small jobs. Many bugs were fixed later.

Even when the programme was ready, they didn't have the right machine to test it. They had no option but to give the maiden demonstration at MITS itself. Finally, it was decided that Allen would go as he was older and appeared mature enough to handle important projects. He flew to Albuquerque for the presentation. It was as if destiny was favouring them. The programme worked perfectly on the company's machine, and they got the contract. Their product was accepted and it resulted in a deal with the company that agreed to distribute the machine as Altair BASIC, virtually accepting their imprint on it. Allen was offered a job at the company, which he accepted. Gates took a leave of absence from Harvard, telling his parents that he would go back if things didn't work out.

They officially formed Microsoft on 4 April 1975 and named the venture 'Micro-Soft' (a combination of 'microcomputer' and 'software'). It was suggested by Paul Allen. They continued to work under the aegis of MITS. However, within a year towards the end of 1976, they became independent of MITS. The hyphen was dropped, and on 26 November 1976, the trade name 'Microsoft' was registered in New Mexico. As their company began to grow, Gates felt no reason to go back to Harvard to get his degree. From then, they continued to develop programming software for a variety of systems and companies. On 1 January 1979 they moved their headquarters to Bellevue, Washington. Commenting on the developments of this time Gates had later remarked, 'We realized the revolution might happen without us. After we saw the article there was no question of where our life would focus.'

MICROSOFT—ON THE FAST TRACK

That's the story of Gates and Allen in the pre-Microsoft days. After forming the company, they had new challenges at hand. As far as the home computer concept was concerned, it was not only a green field but an open level-playing field for the new entrants as there were not too many contenders in the fray. However, establishing a company is easy—the difficult part is maintaining the momentum and growth. That's what the two very young entrepreneurs had begun to realize in their initial years.

In fact, even before starting the company, the two had spent a lot of time introspecting about the viability of their venture. In their position, anybody would have such doubts about the prospects of the proposed company. For Gates, dropping out of the prestigious

Harvard was not easy, and he had had long discussions about it with his parents. He felt grateful to them for supporting him and promised that he would return to Harvard if the project didn't succeed. However, the climate was favouring them. While on the one hand, the two had had the enthusiasm and energy of youth, on the other was the general favourable IT environment.

In hindsight, it appeared to be the right decision. By the end of 1978, their company had managed to grow to twelve employees, including Gates himself. On a photograph taken in December 1978, featuring Microsoft employees, Gates remarked a little defensively in 2009 that it provided indisputable proof that 'your average computer geek from the late 1970s was not exactly on the cutting edge of fashion.' He confessed later that during the initial struggling years, they had had all kinds of concerns. He would be worried about having 'enough money in the bank' to provide for the office expenses and salaries. But since the industry was growing, they had begun to pick up assignments. As Gates's mother was an active social worker and associated with many organizations, they were able to increase their business contacts. It was this avenue that led them to their first major deal that not only changed the fortune of their company, but put the entire computer industry on a different footing.

IBM Deal—The Game Changer (Not Only for Microsoft!)

The deal has been variously described as the 'Deal of the Century' and even the 'Deal with the Devil.' The kind of impact it has had on the entire computer landscape of the world still evokes interesting reactions. The story goes like this. Gates's mother, Mary Maxwell Gates, was a community leader and served on the United Way Charity Board, of which the incumbent IBM chairman, John Opel, was also a member. Through the IBM contact, Gates had been hoping to get some business related to the area in which they had experience—BASIC programming. However, by some oversight in IBM's 'briefing books' Microsoft was listed as a major developer of 'operating systems'. Around this time, since IBM had been looking for an O/S for their newly-developed home computer, they decided to call Microsoft.

To comprehend the complete picture, let's first have a look at the background of home computers in the 1970s. Following the home computer story, we know that in the original 'trinity' of personal computers launched in 1977, Apple II had taken a lead on Commodore PET 2001 by Commodore International and TRS-80 by Tandy Corporation on account of its accounting software, VisiCalc. It had served to widen the computer's scope and helped to re-position the device as a business application gadget also. Yet a lot more ground needed to be covered. As much buzz had begun to develop around the concept of a home computer, some in IBM too began thinking on these lines. Despite being the big boy (the Big Blue) of the industry, it was a new area for them, created by the invention of the microprocessor. As a result, IBM set up a special team, nicknamed 'the Dirty Dozen' to develop a system to outsmart the 'trinity'. Given its resources and clout, it was able to come up with a machine in the beginning of 1981. However, on account of certain internal issues, it still needed an O/S for this from an outside source. Moreover, as earlier the government had proceeded against the company under the antitrust law, they wished to ward off the image of a 'monopolist'. And thus began the Microsoft story.

As mentioned earlier, by some oversight, Microsoft had been described as a 'major developer of operating systems' in IBM's briefing books. So, IBM decided to try them out. When this request to develop an O/S came through, Gates was quite confused to say the least. Gates referred the IBM people to Gary Kildall of DRI (Digital Research, Inc.), who was a known figure in the field of microcomputers. He had written CP/M (originally Control Programme/Monitor, and later Control Programme for Microcomputers) that was ideally suited for the IBM-PC.

There are different versions as to why things didn't work out between the IBM team and Gary Kildall. According to one, when the IBM team arrived at Kildall's house, they needed to negotiate with his wife and business partner, Dorothy Kildall, as apparently, Kildall was out flying his plane that morning. On the advice of her attorney, Dorothy refused to sign the non-disclosure agreement without Gary's approval. It is said that Gary did arrive around lunch time, but instead of an outright sale, he asked for a royalty arrangement with $10 per copy. Perhaps, as the company had a limited product range, it didn't want to sell its main product outright. In short, they couldn't reach an agreement.

Following these developments, Gates decided to explore other options as he didn't want to lose out on the other business he was hoping to get from IBM. He promised IBM an O/S at the earliest.

Gates was able to make this promise because he felt confident of his own talent, and perhaps also on account of Paul Allen's connection with one Tim Patterson. Allen knew that Patterson at SCP (Seattle Computer Products) had been working on an alternative version of CP/M, which he called QDOS (Quick and Dirty Operating System). Gates suggested to IBM that Microsoft could buy this software and further work on it, tailored to the IBM-PC. As IBM was willing to go with the proposal, Microsoft bought the software from SCP, confident that they could modify it to suit the IBM requirement. Microsoft was able to improvise it and it worked well on the IBM-PC. IBM announced its personal computer in August 1981, and finally the product was ready for shipping towards the end of year. It was to be named IBM PC-DOS.

As yet nobody could fathom, not even Microsoft and IBM, how this deal would play out in the long run. The way it did not only transformed the computer industry but still remains a topic of discussion. Microsoft was able to convince IBM to have exclusive rights over the software, besides the royalty payment per computer chargeable to IBM. It was apparently one innocuous clause in the contract between the two companies that gave Microsoft a huge advantage. As we've seen, besides being a gifted software talent, Gates also had a shrewd business sense. It's said that perhaps Gates's father's experience in drafting contracts for companies also came in handy here. In the contract with IBM, a clause was smartly added that allowed the company to sell the same O/S to other companies too under the name MS-DOS. It was this one line that changed the course of the entire computer industry and placed Gates and Allen among the richest people in the world. So, finally as per the contract with IBM, besides being entitled to a license fee per IBM machine, Microsoft was also free to sell the software to other manufacturers.

Bill Gates recalls that around that time, the companies didn't think much of the software. In many cases, it came free with the equipment. In the eyes of most people, hardware was the 'thing'. Gates said, the companies didn't realize that eventually software would be bigger than the hardware. It was on account of this mindset at the time that IBM didn't pay much heed to the seemingly 'harmless' clause. However, it set off a chain reaction that helped to revolutionize the IT industry and bring computers into every home.

In 1977, Apple Inc. had come out with its Apple II, and then there were other brands too. Apple was vertically integrated, producing its own software and hardware. But IBM-PC was set to take the market head-on because of its reputation and reach. As the popularity of IBM-PC increased, the competition was quick to take notice of this development and keen to take advantage of it. For a host of companies, it could be a gold mine. They started on reverse engineering and were soon ready with the IBM clones. Even for IBM, it was good news. The product was a remarkable success, and in just four years, the company had a $4 billion annual revenue in 1984 from PCs alone, and 6 per cent of its own total revenue, much ahead of Apple.

The 'clone' manufacturers needed an O/S for their machines, and Microsoft's MS-DOS was ideally suited for them. It is estimated that Microsoft licensed MS-DOS to over 70 other companies within a year of the launch of IBM-PC in 1981. It's reported that Compaq was the first to 'reverse engineer' the PC and fast grew to be the world's fastest selling PC maker in the late 1980s and early '90s. Established in 1982, during the second year of its operation, it was able to sell 53,000 PCs, reaching a sale of $111 million. In 1987, its revenue hit the $1 billion mark, taking the shortest time to reach there. Then there were companies like Dell Computers, Hewlett-Packard, Acer, AT&T and others. Demand from all these had begun to add to Microsoft's revenue and resources.

To fully comprehend the growth and success of Microsoft at this juncture, we also need to understand the critical role an O/S plays in a computer. We all know that a computer can be broadly divided into two components: hardware and software. However, the software is further categorized into two types of programmes, O/S and individual software or specific applications. Android, Windows, Linux, etc., are examples of O/S while Photoshop, CorelDRAW, Microsoft Word, Excel, PowerPoint, etc., are examples of specific applications. The O/S remains the most essential component in the machine, providing interface between the user and the computer. It performs a variety of tasks such as file handling, memory allocation and de allocation, task scheduling and process management, etc. Without an O/S, the computer would not run. When it comes to individual applications, a user may install one or another depending upon his individual requirements. And to operationalize an individual programme, it has to be aligned, or made compatible, with a specific O/S.

Thus, given the importance of an O/S in computer operation, the IBM deal had kick started the Microsoft operation like never before. From now on till the turn of the century it was to be a dream run for the company. After about five to six years of entrepreneurship for the duo, the IBM deal had set their company on the fast track of growth. Now there was no looking back, and for Bill Gates, no thoughts of returning to Harvard to get his degree. It was a period of growth, success and consolidation. The foundations that were laid during this time stood the company in good stead in future. The IBM connection gradually helped the company to propel itself into the big league and big money. If the MS revenue was $16,005 in 1976, in a short span of seven years, it had grown to $55 million, and stands at $143 billion as of 2020.

Beyond the 1980s

From this point on, the history of Microsoft is closely entwined with the history of the spread of computers in the world. While on the one hand it borrowed from tradition, on the other, it went on to further enrich it through its own innovations and contributions. Since its strength lay in software, the company's energies came to be focused on developing and further improving programmes for the microcomputer and other machines. We need to clarify here that 'original ideas' are rare— what most people land up doing is to build on existing 'templates', and in due course, refining and improving on them. We need to examine Microsoft's efforts in this light. As software was Microsoft's strength, in the context of the current needs, its energies came to be focused on two key components: operating systems and individual applications that would make home computer more useful for the individuals.

We know that Microsoft's MS-DOS had been well-received in the market, and the company had begun to grow on the back of its success. But to keep the momentum going, they were constantly on the lookout for new ideas. These could come from anywhere. Two new concepts that revolutionized personal computer's operation around this time were the mouse and GUI (Graphic User Interface). Although work on them had been going on for quite some time, the 1970s and early '80s computers, Alto and Star, developed by Xerox PARC, were among the first ones to use them. The earlier computers essentially displayed written texts. The mouse freed the user from excessive use of keyboard command, and GUI with its graphics and icons made the operation more convenient and enriching by adding colour and variety to the screen. Microsoft was able to make its MS-DOS word processor mouse compatible in 1983.

However, the real credit for popularizing them and bringing them into the mainstream goes to the team of Bill Gates of Microsoft and Steve Jobs of Apple Inc. Jobs, who was quite imaginative and generally fired by many original and fresh ideas, saw in GUI the 'next big thing' in personal computers while on a visit to Xerox PARC. He asked Bill Gates, in whose programming capabilities he had had much faith and with whom he had previously worked on Apple II, to collaborate with him in developing software for his new line of computers. 'Well, Steve and I worked together, creating the Mac. We (Microsoft) had more people on it, did the key software for it,' Gates had remarked in an interview with Christiane Amanpour.[4]

Convinced of the potential of GUI, he later incorporated it in his MS-DOS line of software and marketed it as Windows 85. Apple took it to be an infringement of their patent rights and sued Microsoft, but later the matter was resolved between the two. The GUI freed the user from much of keyboard command, and allowed him to access files and data using a mouse to click on 'graphic' icons. It was to be a new 'Window' of experience for the user—thus the name stuck and later became a household name.

The key to Microsoft's success throughout all this time has been its aggressive competitive spirit—not to be deterred by failures, but to rather learn from them. Above all it was the 'focus'. During this time, most of the other tech companies had landed up doing several different things simultaneously. Microsoft, on the other hand, was essentially focused on software and its continuous fine-tuning and upgradation. This gave it an edge over one vital aspect of computer technology. So far, from 1985 onwards, Windows has seen nine major versions and numerous minor ones for different servers and devices. Some were successful, while others were not. But the company plodded on, learning from its mistakes and improving on its products.

Although Windows was first launched in November 1985 under the supervision of Bill Gates, and ran on the original MS-DOS, it would take some time for it to become the dominant product. For the company, it was a process of evolution through trial and error. Among the well-received versions, there have been Windows 95 (referring to the year 1995), Windows XP introduced in October 2001, Windows 7 released in 2009, and finally Windows 10 in 2015. The company announced that Windows 10 would be the last version and only updates on it would follow. Many other versions were part of the learning curve for the company, and since it has remained the flagship product of Microsoft, its progress over time and specific features have been discussed in a separate chapter.

Parallel to the Windows range of systems, Microsoft designed individual applications like Microsoft Word, a word processor, Excel, an accounting software and PowerPoint, a presentation software, during the 1980s to make the home computer more useful for common households. Work had been going on in all these areas for long. By the 1980s, there were about 50 different types of word processors in the market, offering different features and advantages. Similarly, before Excel became the industry standard, there were VisiCalc, SuperCalc and Lotus 1-2-3. In the presentation area, a company called Forethought had developed a software called Presenter, which was purchased by Microsoft in 1987, and was later called PowerPoint.

Given these forays, Microsoft had begun to emerge as the leading software company around this time. In 1984, an IT magazine, *InfoWorld*, had stated that 'Microsoft is widely recognized as the most influential company in the microcomputer software industry. Claiming more than a million installed MS-DOS machines, founder and chairman, has decided to certify MS's jump on the rest of the industry by dominating applications, operating systems, peripherals, and most recently book publishing. Some insiders say MS is attempting to be the IBM of software industry.'[5]

New Era, New Competition

With the turn of the century, a lot had begun to change—not only for the computer industry but also for Microsoft and Bill Gates. On the personal front, much had happened in Gates's life starting the early 1990s. In 1994, he got married to Melinda and began to think afresh about his life's priorities. Ever since his teen years, Gates had been practically working nonstop. In his own words, till the age of 30, he had hardly taken any holiday. Certain amount of fatigue was bound to set in. On the professional front, the antitrust move by the government again had taken its toll. Consequently, he decided to hand over the baton to his long-time associate and friend Steve Ballmer, who was made the CEO on 13 January 2000. Gates remained the chairman and took on the position of chief software architect. He stepped aside in 2006 and Ballmer got a free hand in technology-related matters too, besides general operation. Gates's last full day at the company was 27 June 2008. Subsequently, on 4 February 2014, he stepped down as the chairman of the company and took on the role of technology adviser.

As remarked above, with the turn of the century, the computer industry also turned a corner. On account of fast advancements and opening up of world markets, this was a time of rapid developments in the field. The Internet had connected the world like never before. It was the new connector after the railways and aviation of the earlier times. In this new environment, Ballmer was faced with new challenges. Earlier, Gates had bailed out Apple with a $150 million share buy. And then, new entrants like Google and Amazon had begun to come out with new ideas and products. All these factors combined to make Ballmer re-strategize a lot of operation. He remained at the helm of affairs for 14 years up to 2014, and his performance has been described as mixed by observers. The company didn't flounder and maintained a steady growth, but was often criticized for being outsmarted by the competition in new technology areas.

By this time, Microsoft's flagship products, Windows and Office, had been firmly established and could be safely handled in a 'business as usual' way. The future areas were e-tailing, enterprise services and solutions, social media, cloud computing, artificial intelligence (AI), etc. First, Microsoft needed to see its strengths, and then analyze how much involvement it could afford in new technologies. From 2000 till present, the company has made forays into a few new areas with mixed results. These have included gaming, enterprise services, cloud computing, PC, tablet and phone hardware, and AI. Let's examine them separately.

In the gaming area, the company has had a long experience in developing programmes for computer games. One of the first computer games developed by Gates in 1981 was called 'Donkey' (DONKEY.BAS) that involved hitting donkeys. Since gaming was always a revenue-generating stream, the company came out with Xbox on 15 November 2001. It reached a total sale of 24 million units by May 2006 and 84 million units by June 2014. Another advanced variation, Xbox 360, was released in November 2005, which sold 78.2 million units worldwide as of 30 June 2013. This was in direct competition to Sony's PlayStation 3 and Nintendo's Wii. On 22 November 2013, Xbox One was released, which was a successor to Xbox 360 with an emphasis on Internet-based features. On 10 November 2020, the company released Xbox Series X and Xbox Series S, which are the fourth and fifth Xbox consoles succeeding Xbox One. Overall, the gaming consoles' performance can be ranked as moderate, with more plans of expansion underway.

After the cash cows of Windows and Office, it is the cloud computing Azure Service platform that has been one of the bright spots on the company's balance sheet. In fact, as the power and capabilities of the Internet increased, it dawned on the IT companies that they could provide IT services to organizations without the need of having on-site servers and equipment. This would be economical and have the added advantage of many more value-added services. Thus, was born the concept of cloud computing. The lead in this respect was taken by Amazon, the e-retailer giant, by forming a subsidiary, Amazon Web Services (AWS), in 2002 and later providing cloud computing services under its banner from 2006 onwards. The idea began to catch on, and in April 2008, Google released a preview version of App Engine, which sought to offer cloud computing services through Google-managed data centres. It became generally available to people in November 2011.

Microsoft's entry in these services was through Azure Service platform that was announced in October 2008, with the codename Project Red Dog, and was released in 2010 as Windows Azure. It later became Microsoft Azure in 2014. In view of the growing competition, the company needed the extra push to make a place for itself in this area. But gradually, its efforts have begun to pay off, and currently, it's a major player in this domain. Another major step for Microsoft was the establishment of a chain of its retail stores, Microsoft Store, to sell their own products. The first two stores were opened in 2009 in Scottsdale, Arizona, and Mission Viejo, California, within a week of the launch of Windows 7. Over time, it was able to establish over a hundred stores in the US besides in countries such as Canada, Australia, the UK and Puerto Rico. On 26 June 2020, however, the company announced that it would close all its physical retail stores once the COVID restrictions were lifted, and would transition to a digital-only model.

On the macro scene, one of the major developments of this period was the design change of computer hardware, with many new entrants appearing on the stage. From Apple's iPod making its debut in 2001 and later smartphones with LG Prada in December 2006 and then Apple iPhone in June 2007, it was quite a change of face for the basic computer design. Although Blackberry was a precursor to the smartphone, the new devices heralded a paradigm shift and put the computer in the palm of one's hand. Microsoft made determined efforts to capture the smartphone O/S market. It sought to revamp its aging mobile O/S, Windows mobile, and was able to replace it with Windows phone O/S. To consolidate its position in the mobile market, it acquired Nokia's mobile unit in 2013 for $7 billion. In the PC and tablet market, it made its entry by launching the Surface range of PCs in October 2012. For the company, it was a major event and marked a shift in policy as this range had hardware made by Microsoft itself, and was supported by Windows 8.

It was a fast-changing market scenario, and Microsoft needed to review its priorities and options on a regular basis. It was keeping up with the times, but with respect to mobile phones and their O/S and PC and tablet hardware, there had been much competition in the market. With the company's main focus on software, they remained Microsoft's weak areas. On 19 July 2013, the company stocks took their first major hit since 2000 on the poor showing of both Windows 8 and its Surface tablet. In a single day, over $32 billion was wiped off Microsoft's market capitalization. Again, there was never very encouraging news on the mobile phone front. The company's share in the US smartphone market was a measly 2.7 per cent in January 2016. In early 2015, Microsoft had lost $7.6 billion owing to a drop in demand in its mobile business, and this led to sacking of 7,800 employees.

One business policy often followed by ambitious companies is: either develop a good product yourself or buy a successful product and make it your own. That has been the general trend the computer industry has been following since the beginning. As a consequence, many early competitors of Microsoft had disappeared as they were either bought by other larger companies or crushed by Microsoft itself. But then others kept showing up, keeping Microsoft on its toes. IBM bought Lotus in 1995 in an attempt to compete with Windows and Office; Oracle acquired Sun Microsystems in 2010 to strengthen its Unix-based software eco-system. Novell was crushed by Microsoft in 1995 when it began to compete with Microsoft directly.

Microsoft, in a bid to diversify and strengthen its product line, has continued to acquire products and companies over time. Since is public offering in 1986, it has acquired 217 companies, bought stakes in 64 companies and has made 25 disinvestments. Of these acquisitions, 107 companies were based in the US. In its initial years it made some major acquisitions that included Forethought, the creator of PowerPoint, in 1987, and Hotmail in 1997 for $500 million. Some of its key acquisitions since then include: Flash Communications in 1997, NetGames in 2000, Visio in 1999 for $1.3 billion, Nokia in 2013 for $7.2 billion, Skype in 2011 for $8.5 billion, GitHub in 2018 for $7.5 billion and LinkedIn in 2016 for $26.2 billion.

WINDOWS AND OFFICE—STAR PERFORMERS

No story of Microsoft can be complete without a comprehensive account and analysis of the evolution of Windows and Office software. Ever since the early beginnings, they have been the mainstay of Microsoft's operation, and major revenue earners. With over one billion computers worldwide installed with the software (in a world population of about 7.7 billion), their market progress surely makes for an interesting study. Here's an overview.

Windows

Success of a product is usually a result of a long-drawn-out innovation process over time. If we compare the plane the Wright brothers invented in 1903 with the Boeing 747, we have an idea how a product can progress over time. In light of this, the Windows of today is a far cry from the original MS-DOS of 1981 and the Windows of 1985. After the success of the first MS-DOS, the company had embarked on a journey to improve upon the basic system. With a handful of competitors in the market, each was keeping an eye on the other regarding new developments. This sense of competition contributed in a big way to the evolution of many products.

When Steve Jobs of Apple made a visit to the Xerox PARC research facility, he was quite taken in by the concept of GUI developed by the engineers there. He wished to incorporate it in his new line of Macintosh systems, and thus asked his old industry colleague Gates to collaborate on this. Gates found in it a powerful idea and later decided to make it a part of his propriety software, MS-DOS. As it was to be a new 'window' of experience with its graphics and icons for the user, the name thus stuck. Here, it's essential to understand that the main difference between DOS and Windows is that while DOS provides a command line or a text-based interface, Windows provides a GUI.

Following this, Jobs took it to be an infringement of Apple's intellectual rights and went to court. After an acrimonious inconclusive legal tussle, in time, the two settled the issue among themselves, and Gates got a free hand to develop Windows the way he wanted.

Starting 1985, many different versions of Windows were introduced over time, but some elements remained constant despite general variations. Windows 1 was launched in November 1985 under the supervision of Bill Gates, and ran on the original MS-DOS. It relied heavily on the mouse before it became the industry standard. It was also the company's first attempt at a GUI amidst heavy controversy over infringement rights of Apple Inc. Since the mouse as an input device was a new feature, the company wanted users to familiarize themselves with it—and to this effect, a game called Reversi was introduced, whereby the user could learn to move the mouse on the screen to activate the icons and graphic elements. The objective was to make the operation more convenient.

The next generation of the system, Windows 2, released in 1987, introduced an enhanced feature called 'Windows overlap' besides allowing 'maximizing' and 'minimizing' of the same. Sophisticated keyboard shortcuts, expanded memory and a control panel were the additional features that have stayed on since then. The newly developed Microsoft Word and Excel too made their appearance for the first time with this version. Windows 3, launched in 1990, offered improved design, higher memory power and better user interface, and achieved broad commercial success, selling over two million copies in the first six months. It also required a hard drive. It was more successful than the earlier versions and challenged Apple's position in the market. It came pre-installed in the Zenith computer—with 256 colour code and multi-tasking, opened new windows of experience for the user.

The next version was Windows 3.1, introduced in 1992, which was also a viable publishing platform with its True Type fonts. For the first time, the game Minesweeper was introduced in the PC environment. It was the first Windows to be distributed on a CD-ROM, and once installed on the hard drive it took up only 10 to 15 megabytes of space. With a facelift, it also offered a special version 3.11 Windows for Workgroups, with integrated peer-to-peer networking bundled with it.

From Windows 95 began the era of Windows supremacy. It was introduced with much hype with a massive advertising campaign, using the Rolling Stones' 'Start Me Up' to introduce the start button for the first time. A few months later, it was followed up with another ad campaign featuring *Friends* stars Matthew Perry and Jennifer Aniston. It also incorporated the concept of 'plug-and-play' to allow gaming, which was however not totally successful. The task bar appeared for the first time besides the Internet Explorer. But then, unlike later editions, the Internet Explorer here was not installed by default and required 'Windows 95 Plus' pack. Windows 95 also introduced new features such as support for native 32-bit environment and long-file names of up to 255 characters. It was extremely successful and practically became a fixture on the PC desktops all over.

The success of Windows 95 enthused the engineers to add some more features in the next version in 1998. It came with Internet Explorer 4 (IE4), Outlook Express, Windows Address Book, Microsoft Chat and NetShow Player, which was later replaced by Media Player 6.2 in its second edition the following year. This new version was the Windows Driver Model with support for USB composite devices, ACPI, hibernation, multi-monitor configurations and integration with IE4. It also introduced the navigation back-and-forth button and the address bar in Windows Explorer.

By the turn of the century, however, the Windows PC system was all set to change. In view of the changing market conditions, the move had been afoot for some time. From 1980 onwards, besides households, there was an increasing demand of microcomputers from small and medium businesses too. To address this market, Microsoft had launched a parallel line of O/S called Windows NT (new technology) in 1993. It was aimed at power users and those engaged in business activities. So, it was initially designed for workstations and servers, but over time, was expanded to include general-purpose home computers.

Windows ME, released in September 2000, was an outcome of this development. It was the last system in the DOS line and incorporated some 'enterprise' features of Windows 2000 released earlier in the year. It included Internet Explorer 5.5, Windows Media player 7, and the then newly introduced Windows Movie Maker software to facilitate video editing. But then due to some basic flaws, it failed to install properly and proved buggy. On the whole, it wasn't well received in the market.

Windows 2000 was the next in line, on whose

new elements and advancements later O/S were to be developed. It branched into a family of four software: Professional, Server, Advanced Server and Datacenter Server. Its release stretched from February 2000 onwards with Datacenter being re-released in September the same year. However, the home computer line O/S was to be further developed based on its first software called Professional. It was aimed for the business segment along with the domestic market. This software, besides other consumer-line features, introduced automatic updating and support for hibernation—new features for enhanced performance. It was regarded as the 'enterprise-twin' of the ME version and later formed the basis of Windows XP.

The new version Windows XP came to be a favoured edition of the PC Windows group. The company had been trying to enlarge the scope of the PC's O/S by including more enterprise features and it succeeded with Windows XP. Launched in October 2001, it brought both the enterprise mode and the consumer line under one roof. User-friendly elements such as start menu and task bar got a visual overhaul along with introduction of other visual effects. Clear types were introduced to make for easy reading on the LCD screen and facility for CD burning was a new addition. With features such as AutoPlay for CDs, automatic updates and recovery tools, it scored over other versions. It became extremely popular and has had the longest successful run, with three major updates till April 2014, testifying to its general appeal.

However, despite its extreme popularity, security remained an issue with this version as it would get turned off automatically, and also proved to be a boon for the hackers. To counter this complaint of security issue, Bill Gates himself supervised a 'Trustworthy Initiative' with a number of elements and updates that would fortify it against attacks. In the market for six years, it was replaced by Windows Vista in January 2007. Despite all the research and innovation that had preceded it, Windows Vista was not able to make its mark in the market. To counter the 'security threat' the company had perhaps swung to the other extreme. It made the version app-heavy, requiring user account control and user permission to allow for changes or decline, which was an outcome of 'trustworthy computing'. It made the operation slow and cumbersome. As many old PCs ran on Windows XP or earlier versions, it didn't go well with the consumer. Microsoft was even sued on account of its buggy operation. Media Play II and Internet Explorer 7 (IE7) debuted on this. However, for gamers it included Media Direct X 10 technology. Anti-spyware, speed recognition, DVD maker and photo gallery were some of the new features introduced in this. It was the first Windows to be distributed on DVD. Later, a version with Media Player was created in response to antitrust investigations. On the whole, it proved to be a weak link in a strong chain of Windows systems.

Somewhat disconcerted by its reception, the company's tech team proceeded to remove the flaws, and soon had a winner at hand—Windows 7. It was what Windows Vista should've been. The engineers had learnt from some of their earlier mistakes and had come out with a more streamlined version. Windows 7 was launched in October 2009. With a less 'dialogue-box overloaded' interface, it was crammed with many user-friendly features. It was faster, more stable and easier to use. To address possible antitrust issues, it came with a pre-installed Internet Explorer. A box allowing user to choose between different browsers was also introduced. Till date, it has proved to be one of the most successful Windows versions.

With the new movement towards touch-screen mode, Microsoft too decided to incorporate some of its elements in its subsequent releases. Windows 8 was launched in October 2012, and was radically different from the earlier versions. It dispensed with the start menu and button, and brought in touch screen, with a tiled interface of live icons replacing a list of programmes and icons. Faster than the previous version, it also supported faster USB 3.0 devices. Windows Store was introduced, and programmes could still be installed from other iterations of Windows. However, many users felt more comfortable with the mouse and keyboard features and didn't take to it. So, the company introduced 8.1 in October 2013 offering them a choice.

The next and the last in the line was Windows 10 with which the system reached its culmination. It incorporated many user-friendly features and was enthusiastically accepted by people. Released in 2015, it introduced many features ranging from an updated start menu, Cortana, a virtual assistant for the desktop versions, Action Centre incorporating notifications and quick access to settings to a new Web browser, Microsoft Edge, improved multi-tasking to updated built-in apps. From 2015, a range of Windows 10 versions have been released. The company announced that this was to be the last Windows system and there would be updates available from time to time.

According to gs.statcounter.com, as of January 2021 Windows had a total market share of 76.26 per cent in the PC market. While O/SX had a market share of 16.91 per cent, Chrome OS was at 9.65 per cent during this time. Against these, Linux's share was at 1.91 per cent. It is estimated that in 2020, a total of 275.15 million PCs were shipped around the globe. The installed base of PCs worldwide from 2015 to 2019 is 1.5 billion PCs as reported by Statista.

Microsoft Word

With further progress being made in computer technology in the late 1970s, a greater emphasis had also fallen on the development of a smarter word processor. Producing a 'killer application' had been the dream of many a computer engineer. By the 1980s, there were about 50 different types of word processors in the market, offering different features and advantages. The most successful processor around this time was WordStar, that offered automatic mail merging and controlled 25 per cent of the market. In time, it found stiff competition, first from WordPerfect, owned by Corel, and later from Microsoft Word. In the late 1980s and early '90s, WordPerfect had become the dominant word processing software because of its many plus points like macro capabilities, 'reveal codes' features and high-quality support. But then Microsoft was no pushover. Gradually, WordPerfect began losing ground to Microsoft Word—first, because it was late with its first Windows version, and then Microsoft's general strategy to bundle applications with Windows. WordPerfect was first sold to Novell, and then to Corel in 1996. In the meantime, Microsoft Word had stolen a march over it to become the most in demand word processor. WordPerfect has continued to enjoy some support in the legal fraternity, but has negligible market shares today.

Such was the situation when Microsoft entered the market in 1983 with a word processor that ran not on MS-DOS but on Xenix. Xenix was a variation of Unix that Microsoft had earlier licensed from AT&T. It was released as Multi-Tool Word for Xenix Systems. Over time, different versions were created to suit individual requirements of specific OEMs. So, between 1983 and

2019, there have been a variety of Word programmes—the major ones have included: versions for IBM-PC on DOS in 1983, Apple Classic Mac OS and AT&T Unix PC in 1985, Atari ST in 1988, OS/2 and MS Windows in 1989, SCO Unix in 1994, and Mac OS (formerly OSX) in 2001. As new technologies and products continued to appear, Microsoft was quick to develop Word versions for Android and iOS platforms too.

Overall, there have been about 16 versions for Windows, 14 for classic Macintosh and 8 for MS-DOS, besides some others. With a view to upgrade its features and enhance user experience, it has continued to introduce ever new features. These have ranged from task pane, new XML-based file format, XML data bag, content control, contextual tabs, file format docx and ribbon-like feature to select page layouts, besides facility to insert diagrams and images to shape formats faster.

Microsoft Excel

What Word is to writers, Excel is to accountants. And like many other applications, both have emerged out of a long process of improvements and modifications.

Their popularity today is indicative of the value they carry. A look at the history of its evolution affords us interesting insights into its development. In this respect, some initial work had been done in the early sixties by Richard Mattessich, business economist and emeritus professor at the University of British Columbia. Later the real breakthrough came with the development of LANPAR by Rene K. Pardo and Remy Landau in 1970. Although there was some dispute about its patenting, the programme became the de facto system for a variety of calculations and tabulating activities. Soon it came to be used by leading companies like Bell Canada and AT&T, besides 18 other local and national telephone companies, for their budgeting activities. But then, with advancement in computer technology, many new possibilities were in store.

As work in this direction had been going on in different quarters, one may say that the concept of an electronic spreadsheet came into its own with the launch of Apple II in 1977. The system incorporated a new spreadsheet called VisiCalc which had been developed by Bob Frankston and Dan Bricklin of Software Arts. This helped the home computer rise to a new level. With this new application the microcomputer was transformed from a gaming device into a serious personal and business tool. VisiCalc came to be regarded as a 'killer application' and its demand shot up with a sale of 70,000 copies in the first six years, and over a million in its history. It set off a chain reaction, and Apple II's popularity prompted IBM to set up its own unit and produce its first PC to cash in on the new growing opportunities.

The next to appear on the scene was SuperCalc, which was an improvement on VisiCalc. Microsoft, an emerging software company at the time, couldn't ignore such developments, and a year later, introduced Multiplan. It was still a step ahead of others and was targeted towards systems running CP/M, MS-DOS, Xenix and many others. However, competition in this respect was heating up around this time and the appearance of Lotus 1-2-3 introduced a new dimension to the scenario in 1983. Developed by Lotus software in 1983, it was ahead of all the others.

Looking for a large market share, Lotus sought affiliation with IBM. Although IBM had a contractual agreement with VisiCalc and was shipped simultaneously with IBM-PC, the company was inclined towards a tie-up because of its obvious advantages.

First, the name referred to three-fold product use: it could be used as a spreadsheet, graphics package and database manager. As it had support from IBM (like MS-DOS earlier), it was set to sway the market. Another novelty that Lotus introduced was a graph maker that could make several types of graphs, including pie charts, bar graphic or line charts. It was a new revolution in accounting software and soon began to edge out all the other rivals to become the ruling product. Microsoft's Multiplan tried to cope with it but was not successful. Despite having sold over a million copies, it was being outsold, and in the mid-1980s and much of the '90s, Lotus had become the product of choice, so much so that in the market, people would ask for the 'Lotus PC'. According to Bill Gates, the main reason for Multiplan lagging behind was that they had tried to align it with too many ports. In all, there were about 100 different versions of Multiplan around that time.

But then, as the luck would have it, the wind started blowing in Microsoft's favour. While on the one hand, Lotus had been working on improving Multiplan, on the other, it began to run into rough weather. Microsoft released its improved version of Multiplan as Excel in

1985 for Apple Macintosh, which for the first time had a graphical interface. In 1987, Excel 2.0 was released with Windows. During this time, Lotus had begun to suffer some technical issues in converting from macro assemblers to a more portable 'C' language. As Excel was part of Windows, which was a preferred O/S, its popularity soared. Lotus began to lose ground, and gradually Excel began to improve its market share to dominate the market.

In all, over 13 major versions of Microsoft Excel for Windows have been introduced in the market so far, each a step up from its previous iteration. From the early basic stage, it has gone on to induct features such as toolbars, drawing capabilities, outlining, multi-sheet workbooks, interface for VBA developers, user forms and data validation in earlier editions to enhanced clipboard, pivot charts, model user forms, sparkling graphics, pivot table slicers, single-document interface and charting enhancements, besides many other features.

Microsoft PowerPoint

Microsoft acquired LinkedIn in 2016 for $26.2 billion, while Facebook had acquired WhatsApp in 2014 for

$19 billion. Compared to this, buying PowerPoint for $14 million in 1987 appears to have been a bargain. The times were different, yet the difference is huge. According to analysts, the deal has perhaps proved to be a bigger money spinner than most of Microsoft's other products or acquisitions. Initially sceptical about the purchase, Bill Gates's acquisition today is installed on over a billion computers worldwide, and remains one of the most formidable software ever created.

A business presentation in pre-PowerPoint days was a different story altogether. Earlier, a business meeting meant distribution of certain documents to the members, which would be followed by discussion with each member making his notes and speaking in turn. Over time, business houses graduated to chart presentations, and then slide projections when they came into vogue. As mentioned in Chapter II, contributions in this respect, however, were made by companies such as Trollman, Genigraphics (division of GE), Dicomed and others that had devised computer workstations on which presentations graphics software could run a large number of slides. But then it was an expensive and cumbersome process that only large corporations could afford. For others, a smarter economical option was on the way. With the advent of microcomputers, especially PCs, the whole game of business presentations underwent a dramatic change. So in the early eighties, a large number of companies had begun to develop presentation software, and by 1987, Microsoft too had initiated its own project to this effect.

Given the market situation, the company thought an acquisition would be a better choice. Out of the two options, Jeff Raikes of Microsoft preferred Forethought's offering, Presenter, because of its clear advantage of overhead presentations. Initially, Gates was somewhat sceptical about the acquisition and had thought that the presentation application could be a feature of Word, not a separate product in itself. He gradually became convinced otherwise and Forethought was acquired by Microsoft in July 1987. Forethought had initiated a project in 1984 with an aim to develop a presentation application for Apple Macintosh and Microsoft Windows. The work progressed satisfactorily and they were able to produce a major design specification document for Apple. Based on the positive outcome of this, Forethought was assured funding by Apple in January 1987. By April 1987, they were ready with PowerPoint for Macintosh, and the first product run of 10,000 units was sold. Subsequently, in July, the company was acquired by Microsoft. All through, the product had been called Presenter, but was later named PowerPoint, as 'Presenter' had already been registered by someone else. Gaskins, the lead developer, called it PowerPoint as it assured certain power to the individual presenter and sounded 'powerful'.

Following this, in mid-1988, a new PowerPoint 2.0 was released for Apple that went colour (from the earlier black and white) with 35-mm slides. Although initially received well in the market, PowerPoint was not able to acquire the desired share in view of many competing entities. One major reason for this was that as yet Windows with PowerPoint had not been released and most of the PCs in the market ran on MS-DOS, which used the presentation software of Harvard Graphics and Lotus Freelance Plus. Later, when the first version of PowerPoint 2.0 for Windows was released, the scene began to change. It was able to ride the popularity wave of Windows like many other products, took a lead over Apple and never looked back. Since then, its worldwide market share has been estimated at over 90 per cent and remains unchallenged.

Following subsequent changes and improvements, PowerPoint today is available in 102 languages, ranging from Arabic, Assamese and Bulgarian to Polish, Punjabi and Turkish. Compatible versions for Android, iOS have also been released, besides others.

THE PROGRAMMER AND ENTREPRENEUR

Behind the success of any big venture, there are always some incredibly strong-willed people, determined to run the course, and whatever be the challenges or obstacles, they do not let go of their dreams half-way. Intelligence, vision, hard work, maturity in dealings, money management—a whole host of qualities come into play here. And above all, of course, there is the role of destiny too. It's difficult to say if Bill Gates was blessed with all these qualities, but one thing is evident: he did possess many such traits that made him the richest man in the world at just 40. Then there's the role of Paul Allen too, whose personality study we'll take up in another chapter.

Overall, the success story of Microsoft is, in a way,

also the study of Bill Gates's personality, as he was the chief architect of the 'house that Windows built'. To understand the success of Microsoft, we need delve deeper into his personality, which has been under public gaze and scrutiny ever since he started making waves.

Professional Journey

In the previous chapters, we've touched upon Bill Gates's early life and influences. Here, our focus is on his personality and the traits that helped in contributing to the success and growth of Microsoft.

In the case of Bill Gates, it's difficult to separate his personal life from professional, especially in the first 30 years of his life. By his own admission, he was quite 'fanatical' about work in the initial years of the company's growth. The very fact that he was able to create a marketable product at 17 and form a company — that is still one of the largest in the world — at just 20 points to a certain determination in his character.

Some of his associates felt that, unlike other teenagers, he had missed out on his youth. Ed Roberts, the co-founder of MITS, the company that gave Bill

Gates his first big break, once remarked, 'He's kind of like Elvis Presley. He never got to grow up.'[6] Steve Jobs, another associate had remarked, 'He'd be a broader guy if he had dropped acid once, or gone off to an ashram when he was younger.' During this time, by his own admission, he scarcely took a holiday. Sometimes he would be up the whole night working at the office. The story goes that one day, when an early-morning employee entered the office, she was surprised to see 'someone' sleeping on the floor. It was Bill Gates! In the beginning, Gates would himself supervise and read every word of the code before it was shipped, and would even rewrite wherever he thought it necessary. He once said in an interview, 'If some friend called me, I didn't have time. I was super busy. I never took a day off in my 20s. I'm still fanatical, but now I'm a little less fanatical. I play tennis. I play bridge. I spend time with my family. I drive myself around town in a normal Mercedes.' Over time, he's moved on to a 'normal' life.

Since he himself was a workaholic, Gates expected a certain degree of commitment and dedication from his staff members too. In the early days, when the company needed to keep a control over finances, he was more careful about his staff's performance. By his own admission, he would even memorize his employees' car number plates to keep a tab on their arrival and departure timing. There has also been much talk about his temper outbursts. Impatient with inadequate replies, he would burst out, 'That's the most stupid idea I've ever come across', 'Someone is not thinking here' or a sarcastic comment, 'Oh, I would think it over the weekend.'

His compatriot and partner, Paul Allen, recalls the screaming matches they would have from time to time over disagreements about certain company policies or new ventures. Gates would say that he was very hard on himself. He would get irritated with himself when he would begin to pursue some 'stupid or unworkable idea.' 'How can I be so stupid to think of such an idea,' he would muse later. However, as the company grew and became financially stable, Gates began to relax somewhat and pursue other interests in life.

Apart from hard work, another major attribute that worked in his favour was his keen business sense — being alive to current market trends, showing agility in operation and acquisitions, along with hard-nosed negotiating skills. He exhibited these qualities right from the beginning, from the time he developed software for Altair along with Allen in the famous deal with IBM, to conducting himself in the dispute with Steve Jobs over the use of GUI. Around this time, some writers rather uncharitably described Microsoft's policy with regard to acquisitions and buy-outs as 'Extend, Embrace, Extinguish.' It meant that the company would acquire a rather fledgling product from the market, make necessary modifications as per its own needs and make it completely its own, thus 'extinguishing' the original product. This was all part of the hard-drive vision of Bill Gates.

Partners, Friends and Frenemies

From a business point of view, Bill Gates has had three important relationships: Paul Allen, Steve Ballmer and Steve Jobs. It would be helpful here to analyze his relationship with each separately.

Paul Allen

There have been other 'twin' partners in the tech business—Hewlett and Packard of HP, Steve and Steve of Apple Computer, Sergey Brin and Larry Page of

Google—but the relationship of Gates and Allen has had few parallels in the business world. Given the difference in their personalities, it's not too surprising that it didn't last a lifetime. The two had their good and bad moments, but in the long run, it didn't last as it should have. We've already seen how the two virtually grew up together in the computer rooms at school and university, but as time progressed, there was a gradual cooling off.

Allen was about three years older than Gates and fond of reading, and so his horizon was much wider. As a result, Gates was generally benefitting from the association, and even felt a little grateful to Allen for keeping him by his side. Nevertheless, there's no doubt that personality wise, both were very different people. And as they began to mature, the differences became more noticeable. Gates admits, that though being far ahead of his times, Allen was not happy being a manager and confined to a desk. He had many diverse interests, and he sought a much larger, broader life; the outdoors excited him. In all likelihood, this was one of the main reasons for them drifting apart.

Gates was cast in a different mould. He was happy giving himself to computers and wanted to build a great company, working till late at night at office. 'Gates would say, I wonder what it's like to run a Fortune 500 company,' recalls Allen. 'And I'd say, "I don't know".' As there was pressure to build the company and keep up with the competition, often, the two would land up having arguments over work-related issues. 'Gates has a very intense discussion style,' says Allen. 'My style is very much more logical.'

In April 2011, Allen, gave an interview to Lesley Stahl for CBS 60 Minutes[7] after the publication of his book *Idea Man: A Memoir by Co-founder of Microsoft*. She described it as a 'bitter book', referring to the difficult relationship Gates and Allen shared. Allen had commented on Gates's aggressive style that could at times be 'browbeating, leading to personal verbal attacks.' He recalls incidents when the two would end up having 'screaming matches' which would go on for hours. 'It's really exhausting,' says he. 'I was too angry and proud to tell Gates point blank that "sometimes working with you is being in hell".' He remembers how Gates would always be pushing him to work more, even more than he would others. Gates, on the other hand, had other concerns. In the initial stages, there was also the question of cash flow and

Gates would be worried about having enough money in the bank to pay salaries. He gradually began to feel as if the responsibility of running the company rested on his shoulders, and that he had been undertaking a greater burden of the work. However, the precipitating moment came after Allen was diagnosed with Hodgkin's lymphoma in 1982.

It was a difficult time for Allen. And as he was unable to contribute substantially towards work, he felt he was becoming a liability to the company. He recalls, 'As I was passing by Gates's office one night, I heard Gates and Steve Ballmer talking about me,' said Allen in his interview to Lesley Stahl. 'They were basically talking about diluting my share almost to nothing.' For him, it was a very 'shocking and disheartening moment'. 'I was perhaps in the middle of my radiation therapy.' He said that he burst down and confronted them as they had been planning to rip him off. Gates perhaps felt embarrassed by his behaviour, and later that night, sent Ballmer to his house to apologize.

Given these developments Allen, thought that the time had come for him to leave. Then there came up the contentious issue of ownership. With both Allen and Gates being 50 per cent partners, Allen rightfully thought of himself as half-owner of the company. It's said that Gates asked him to give him an additional part of his shares as Gates 'had done almost everything on BASIC'. On the other hand, both knew that in the O/S development for IBM's PC, Allen had had a larger contribution. However, Allen agreed to split the shares 60:40 in his partner's favour. Gates later negotiated the deal to a 64:36 split. The company had been doing well, and Gates had had great plans for the future and felt quite confident of high growth. Against this backdrop, Gates was tempted to increase his holding, and in 1983 again tried to buy out Allen at $5 per share, but Allen refused and left the company, practically one-third owner of Microsoft. When Microsoft went public on 13 March 1986, with IPO of $21 per share, by the end of the day, the share value had risen to $35.50. It made Allen's investment worth six times what Gates was offering him at the time of separation. In 1983, when he left Microsoft, Allen could envision the skies opening up for him. He had been declared cancer-free, and with the kind of fortune he had in his hands, he was free to pursue his dreams.

Steve Ballmer

It appears that as the company started to grow, Gates had begun to get somewhat disenchanted with Allen's attitude towards work. He was looking for an alternate support, which he sought in his old Harvard friend Steve Ballmer. Ballmer was inducted into Microsoft as the 30th employee and the first manager in June 1980. In the beginning, it was great going for the two and this state lasted for quite some time. He was the best man at Gates's wedding in 1994, and people talked of their 'mind-meld' and described their relationship as a 'virtual marriage'. However, when one works in a high-pressure environment, it's not unusual for close co-workers to develop some kind of friction. And this is precisely what began to plague their old relationship.

As Gates had begun to feel rather fatigued by the onerous responsibilities of work and sought some relief, he decided to divest himself of some of his duties in 2000. He was happy that Ballmer was willing to accept the position of CEO, and on 13 January 2000, was designated so. Gates stepped aside, assuming the new role of chief software architect. Although Ballmer was the new CEO, he had general management duties, while the technological 'vision' was reserved for Gates. It was only in 2006 when he resigned from this position that Ballmer got full control over technology-related matters.

Although the two had been rather close for a long time, it has been reported that there was tension surrounding the transition of authority. It is said that on one occasion, there was much screaming and shouting over Ballmer defending some employees, with Gates leaving the meeting in a huff. The relationship was gradually losing its old-time warmth and camaraderie. Ballmer even remarked that once Gates left, 'I'm not going to need him for anything. That's the principle. Use him, yes, need him, no.' A few months after Ballmer had resigned from Microsoft, a *Vanity Fair* magazine profile in October 2014 had said that the two no longer speak to each other due to differences over Ballmer's resignation. In an interview in November 2016, Ballmer revealed that the two had 'drifted apart', adding that while earlier the two had had 'brotherly relations', this rift came because of his push into the hardware business, especially smartphones.

Steve Jobs

The times were such that everybody was looking over each other's shoulders to see what the other person was up to. The industry was becoming increasingly competitive. Both Bill Gates and Steve Jobs had entered the arena around the same time—Gates set up his shop in 1975 and Jobs in 1976. In the words of Steve Wozniak, the co-founder of Apple Inc., their focus had been more on the hardware—for software, they could even seek outside help. While Apple was a vertically integrated company, Microsoft was essentially focused on software. Gates and Jobs were in the same field and had needed each other's help from time to time. Their association has been described as a love—hate relationship—they were 'frenemies' of sorts!

As Apple's main focus was on hardware, for more specialized software they often sought outside help. Microsoft was a rising star and thus the two companies often collaborated with each other. Although Microsoft's commitment towards MS-DOS PCs was greater, it had been developing individual applications and other specific software for a variety of companies. Apple was again a valued customer. Microsoft helped in the software designing of Apple II and, by Gates's own account, he had 'more people than Apple' who worked on the development of software for their new line of Macintosh computers.

It was after the Mac project that their relationship nosedived on the issue concerning the use of GUI in MS-DOS. Steve Jobs thought that since he had used it first, he had the intellectual right over it, though originally, the concept had come from the Xerox PARC lab. Following this, Apple sued Microsoft, but since there were many legal lacunae, the case didn't progress far. On account of this, it was a see-saw relationship between the two, both often accusing each other, yet continuing to collaborate. On account of the GUI issue, Jobs accused Gates of breach of trust. 'They just ripped us off completely, because Gates has no shame,' said Jobs, as described in self-titled biography, *Steve Jobs: A Biography*, by Walter Isaacson.[8] To this Gates replied, 'If he believes that, he really has entered into one of his own reality distortion fields.' In Gates's opinion, Jobs was 'fundamentally odd' and 'weirdly flawed as a human being.'

This love—hate relationship continued all their lives. Despite his criticism, Gates thought well of Jobs's design sense and remarked that Jobs 'never knew much about technology, but he had an amazing instinct for what works.' In his view, Jobs was a great marketing guy, a 'super salesman', and nothing more. In 1996, Jobs appeared in a PBS documentary *Triumph of the Nerds* and vented his old grudge against Gates saying that Microsoft makes 'third-rate products'. Yet the two soon put their past behind them and, in 1997, Gates decided to bail out Jobs when Apple was in deep financial trouble. Microsoft bought $150 million worth of the Apple stock, besides additionally helping them out with a broad cross-licensing contract. According to this agreement, whereby Microsoft promised the support of Microsoft Office for Mac for five years, Apple consented to make Internet Explorer the default browser on their Mac computers.

Despite this off-and-on bonhomie, Jobs was quite caustic in his comments when Gates decided to leave Microsoft. He said, 'Gates is basically unimaginative and has never invented anything, which is why I think he's more comfortable now in philanthropy than in technology.' Still, from the other side, there were kind words. In the famous joint D5 conference interview in May 2005, Gates said, 'I'd give a lot to have

Steve's taste.'[9] And Jobs once said, 'I admire him for the company he built — it's impressive — and I enjoyed working with him. He's bright and actually has a good sense of humour.' Gates's comments after Jobs's death suggest he didn't harbour any bitterness against him: 'I respect Steve, we got to work together. We spurred each other on, even as competitors. None of that (what he said) bothers me.'

However, both in the long run proved to be major wealth creators. The companies they created continue to vie with each other for a greater market share of their products.

BILL GATES: FAMILY AND OTHER ENGAGEMENTS

Though Bill Gates had got busy in building his company in his early youth, it didn't mean he didn't have any other interest in life. As his company began to stabilize in the mid-1980s, he had even begun to think of marriage. Melinda first caught his eye when they sat next to each other at a 1987 Expo-trade dinner at New York. 'He was funnier than I thought,' says she. Four months into her job at Microsoft, she had had a certain impression of the boss, which was to change over time. A few weeks later, when the two bumped into each other in the company's parking lot, he asked her out. Gates being a busy man was used to schedule his appointments, and suggested a two-week later date for going out. Melinda wondered if this hard-nosed tech genius had a romantic side to him at all, and said he should ask her again near that date. Gates got the hint and called her after an hour or so and asked if they could go out that evening. She agreed and gradually, over subsequent meetings, they began to develop a fondness for each other. What struck Gates about Melinda was her forthrightness, and sense of independence. (She was not intimidated by the boss!) In fact, Gates would often joke in company that his wife was more educated than him. Interestingly, he got an honorary degree from Harvard when the university felicitated its most successful dropout in 2007.

Melinda

Melinda Gates was born Melinda Ann French on 15 August 1964 in Dallas to Raymond Joseph French, an engineer and house-rentals agent, and Elaine Agnes Amerland, a home maker. From the beginning, she was a bright student, usually on top of her class in school. Her first introduction to the cyber world happened when her father brought her an Apple II, the most popular PC those days. As her interest in computers grew, she took up computer science later and graduated in Computer

Science and Economics from Duke University, North Carolina. She later joined IBM as an intern, and on the advice of her career counsellor, applied to Microsoft, as she felt she had a better future with it as the company was growing. In a few years at Microsoft, she advanced from marketing manager of multimedia products to general manager of information products.

She got married to Bill Gates in 1994, and in their 27 years of marriage, the two have been able to raise three kids, and lead a happy married life. They have three children, Jennifer born in 1996, Rory in 1999 and Phoebe in 2002. According to Melinda, one of the secrets of their successful marriage has been finding the right balance and 'balance in rights' — a sense of equality. She believes one should try to make the relationship as equal as possible for harmony to prevail. The proof lies in the fact that she has been able to persuade one of the richest men in the world to share household chores with her, including washing dishes. He would drop the children at school too. That move got the other mothers at school to exhort their husbands also to follow his example — 'If Bill Gates can do it, why not you!'

Satisfied with the way his business had been shaping, over time, Gates had started to become more of a family man. He had begun the construction of his house in 1988 that took seven years to build and cost $63 million. It is a 50,000 sq ft, seven-bedroom house located at Medina, Washington, and has a 60-ft swimming pool, six kitchens, dining hall for 200 people, and a 20-ft high trampoline room, besides entrance through a private tunnel and other luxuries.

In addition to this, he also has numerous other properties, including a 229-acre horse farm in Rancho Paseana in Rancho Santa Fe, California, and another one at Wellington, Florida, as his daughter Jennifer is an avid equestrian. He also owns about half of the Four Seasons hotel chain. With his priorities changing, from 2000 onwards, he had started getting more involved in philanthropic activities, his commitment towards such projects increasing with every passing year. The COVID-19 pandemic of 2020 has engaged his attention considerably and he's taken many proactive steps to deal with the situation.

Gates and Melinda Gates Foundation

In 1994, Gates started the William H. Gates Foundation. Six years later, he and his wife combined three family foundations and renamed it the Bill and Melinda Foundation to which Gates donated stock worth $5 billion. Its co-chairs have been Bill Gates, Melinda Gates and William H. Gates Sr., with Mark Suzman as the CEO. With Gates Sr. passing away on 14 September 2020, the Foundation now has two co-chairs, Bill Gates and Melinda Gates. Warren Buffet, the owner of Berkshire Hathaway, has now been nominated as one of the three trustees along with Bill and Melinda. As of 2021, it is the largest private endowment fund in the world with a holding of $50.7 billion.

The objectives behind the Foundation are: one, address healthcare issues in the world and reduce extreme poverty; and two, expand educational opportunities in the US and improve access to information technology. During its 20-year journey, it has achieved many a landmark, making a difference in people's life at the ground level. In June 2006, Warren Buffet, the owner of Berkshire Hathaway and the richest man in the world at the time, with a net worth of $64 billion, sought involvement in the Foundation and pledged to contribute a certain amount on an annual basis, with an offering of $1.5 billion in the first year. A unique feature about the Foundation has been its clear emphasis on transparency, conspicuously absent in many other charities of the kind. It allows the benefactors to access information in respect to the areas where their money is being spent.

Since its beginning, it has launched major initiatives and supported worldwide programmes in the areas designated in its mandate. Over time, in areas of education it has granted $20 million to Carnegie Mellon University (CMU) for the Gates Centre for Computer Science that opened in 2009; $20 million to MIT for construction of computer laboratory called William H. Gates Building; $6 million for construction of the Gates Computer Science Building at Stanford University, completed in 1996. Besides these projects, it has also established Cambridge Scholarships with an endowment of $210 million at Cambridge University, on the lines of the Rhodes scholarship, for students from across the world. The Foundation, through its various programmes, has been facilitating bright students' admissions into prestigious universities like Cornell, Harvard and others to foster excellence in education among different sections.

The Foundation's financial inclusion endeavours have helped provide a variety of financial advantages to the marginalized sections surviving on less than $2 a day in many countries. They have helped individuals to create savings accounts besides accessing insurance and other financial services. The Foundation has also made grants to conduct field surveys in the area of microfinance, which include granting of a five-year $3.1 million grant to Pro Mujer Inc., a microfinance network in Latin America and $1.5 million grant to the Grameen Foundation, a US-based NGO working on similar lines in the developing world. It has also given a grant of $5 million to the International Justice Mission (IJM), an organization that works in the area of sex trafficking and slavery. IJM has been quite successful in its efforts through its programme Project Lantern in the city of Cebu in Philippines.

In the agriculture sector, it has been able to start major programmes that have included supporting the International Rice Research Institute located in Philippines to develop a genetically modified rice variant to combat Vitamin A deficiency and donating $146.4 million to Alliance for a Green Revolution in Africa, $777 million to the Global Fund to fight AIDS, tuberculosis and malaria, $334 million for the Medicines to Malaria Venture, $166 million to WHO Nigeria

Country Office, $199.5 million to Clinton Health Access Initiative Inc. and $338.4 million to Global Alliance for TB drug development, among others.

Well-organized water management and sanitation are critical to the health of any community. Through its Water, Sanitation and Hygiene (WASH) programme the Foundation has launched a variety of projects for sanitation and hygiene improvement. Around one billion people in the world have no sanitation facility, with about 600 million in India alone. Since 2011, the Foundation has been funding a variety of projects in India to end the practice of open defecation. In addition, it has also been focusing on developing innovative sanitation techniques for slum dwellers in sub-Saharan and South Asian countries. The challenge in such areas has been to develop systems that are independent of piped water and sewage facilities.

Part of the same programme is the 'Reinvent the Toilet Challenge' launched by the Foundation to focus on developing on-site and off-site water treatment solutions, and to create a toilet that not only removes pathogens from excreta, but also recovers resources such as energy, clean water and nutrients. It has been at work behind the creation of the omni-processor, which is a combustion-based system that converts fecal sludge into energy and drinking water. These initiatives have made a significant difference in improving people's lives in these areas.

But despite a lot of good work and well-meaning initiatives, the Foundation has often come under criticism from different social organizations and certain sections of the media. It has been alleged that the charity favours specific companies and many of its programmes ultimately benefit Microsoft, such as the promotion of IT education in the US. However, overall, its endeavours have been much appreciated, not only in the US but in other parts of the world as well. In 2005, Bill and Melinda Gates, along with musician Bono, were named persons of the year by *Time* for their outstanding charitable work. In 2007, the Foundation was presented with the Indira Gandhi Peace Award by the Indian president Pratibha Singh Patil, and in 2015, Bill Gates and Melinda Gates jointly received India's third-highest civil honour Padma Bhushan and in 2016, then US president Barack Obama conferred on them the Presidential Medal for Freedom for their philanthropic work.

BILL GATES'S FAMILY—ITS VALUE SYSTEM AND INFLUENCES

Childhood is an impressionable age. Children don't just learn from direct teaching but also from their surroundings—by observing how people behave with one another, their value systems, priorities, etc. In this respect, Gates was fortunate to have had strong personalities in both his parents. Upright and God-fearing, well-educated with strong family values and beliefs, they were firmly rooted in strong ethical traditions.

The family attended a dispensation of the Presbyterian Church and Christian values formed part of their general outlook to life. They felt an individual's duty is not only to himself but also to the family and community. There were obligations to be met on both sides, as they were complimentary to each other—no man is an island unto himself. Family was important. One may pursue any number of interests for one's overall development, but not at the expense of important family commitments. So, they had made an important 'no-reading-at-the-dinner-table' rule to encourage familial interaction. The parents had held strong views about community commitments too. It was important to show solidarity with your people around, even if it was for small causes. *Showing up for Life* by Gates Sr. outlines his ideas on the subject. What he had himself learnt from experience and practiced was that 'giving back to society' was important. Show up—whether it's for collecting funds for slum rehabilitation or helping a neighbour clear his driveway in event of a storm.

The family encouraged the children to stay curious and learn from mistakes instead of being scared of them. Sharing his sense of curiosity and wonder with another genius of earlier times, Gates once wrote in his blog, 'When you look across all of Leonardo's many abilities and his few failings, the attribute that stands out above all else was his sense of wonder and curiosity.' He added, 'When he wanted to understand something—whether it was the flow of blood through the heart or the shape of a woodpecker's tongue—he would observe it closely, scribble down his thoughts, and then try to figure it all out.' Gates was so impressed by Da Vinci's achievements that he even bought Da Vinci's 'Codex Leicester' for $30.8 million in 1994, making it one of the most expensive books ever sold. The 72-page document, written between 1506 and 1510, contains Da Vinci's sketches and ideas about subjects like astronomy, mechanics, botany, mathematics and architecture.

One lesson that Gates Sr. had learnt himself and passed on to the next generation was that the reluctance, the diffidence to try out things new is a big stumbling block in one's progress. Always playing safe in life is not an option. It was important to get out of your comfort zone and open yourself to new experiences, new experiments. Even if you fail, you would come away with a bagful of lessons, which would stand you in good stead in the years to come.

The family also believed that simply living a cloistered life indoors was detrimental to the general well-being of an individual. A balance between the indoors and outdoors is necessary, between the classroom teaching and theory and the outdoor practical life. So, during his high school years, Gates was allowed to undertake a programming assignment at a power plant, as both his school headmaster and parents thought that some exposure to professional practical life would do him good.

A lesson from the 'Book of Luke', *New Testament* — 'From those, to whom much is given, much is expected' — had characterized Gates's mother's basic philosophy of life. In time, she passed it on to her children. Gates had said in his 2007 Harvard commencement speech, 'She never stopped pressing me to do more for others.' In this context, he has also talked of a letter his mother had written to his fiancée Melinda in 1993, a little before his marriage, where her advice echoed Voltaire's belief that with great power comes great responsibility. We must recall that around this time, Gates was one of the wealthiest people in the world, and his mother expected him and his wife to do much for others.

Apart from the direct teachings and lessons that are imparted to children, the individual personalities of the parents also affect their overall behaviour. To have more comprehensive view of influences on Bill Gates, it would be helpful to study the individual personalities of both his parents.

Mary Maxwell Gates

Mary Maxwell Gates, Gates's mother, was born on 5 July 1929 in Seattle to a banker father James Willard Maxwell and his wife Adele Thomson. Her grandfather too had been a prominent banker and was the president of National City Bank of Seattle from 1911 to 1929. After receiving a degree in education from the University of Washington (UW), Seattle, in 1950, she married William H. Gates Sr., an Arts and Law graduate of the same university, in 1951.

Soon after her marriage, she worked for some time as a teacher and then got involved in a range of civic and community activities. She also served on the Board of United Way Charity. Her philanthropic work was not limited to the state but extended to the entire country. In 1975, when Governor Evans appointed her to the Board of Regents to UW, she led a movement to divest the University of its holding in South Africa to protest against apartheid. At her memorial service after her death in June 1994, the then UW president William P. Gerberding spoke of her capacity for 'infectious, effervescent joy' and her 'largeness of purpose and spirit'. 'She was a luminous presence and a powerful influence at this University and in community,' he said, 'She was a catalyst, a person who sought and often found common ground when it was not apparent to others. Everyone trusted and respected her judgement. Her leadership was subtle, but it was steady.'

In this respect, we also need to recognize the contribution of Gates's family in the building of Microsoft. His mother was an active community person who was associated with many organizations. In the early years of Microsoft, Gates would often accompany her on her assignments to different companies to promote his business. The fact that she and John Opel of IBM were on the United Way Charity Board together considerably helped Microsoft in building their initial association with IBM, which proved to be a great bonanza for them later. Much of his philanthropic spirit has been imbibed from his mother, as mentioned previously; she always exhorted him to do more and more for others much before Microsoft came into existence and became large enough to establish a major philanthropic organization.

William Henry Gates, Sr.

William Henry Gates Sr., Bill Gates's father, was born on 30 November 1925 in Bremerton, Washington, to William Henry Gates I and Lillian Elizabeth Rice. His father ran a furniture store in the town. After graduating from Bremerton High School, Gates Sr. enlisted in the US army and served the force for three years. After World War II, having been discharged honourably in 1946, he joined the University of Washington, earning a BA in 1949 and a Law degree in 1950. In 1951, he married Mary Ann Maxwell, who attended the same university.

Bright and intelligent, it was no surprise that Gates Sr. was able to distinguish himself in the legal profession, earning much recognition and respect in an over four-decade-long career. He was a prominent member of the legal fraternity, widely respected and looked up to for judicious counsel. He served as the president of Seattle King County Bar Association and also of Washington State Bar Association. He served on the boards of important institutions, including the Greater Seattle Chamber of Commerce. In 1995, he founded the Technology Alliance whose mission was to expand technology-based employment in the state of Washington.

Like Gates's mother, his father too proved to be a strong role model for him in the long run. He has high praise for his father whose qualities he greatly admired. Gates Sr. was much alive to his community and its issues, always concerned about how well it was educating the younger generation, both academically and ethically. He volunteered for a variety of social welfare activities. Gates particularly singles out his father's role in reforms and improvements in legal system. 'The Bar was certainly the biggest thing he did,' says he. 'He had a lot of stuff about judicial reform and malpractice insurance for lawyers.' However, being a self-made man and a self-effacing person, he always preferred to work with consensus rather than being too opinionated. According to Gates, he could've been a judge but decided against it, as his law firm at that time was in a situation he didn't want to leave it in. 'I always thought he would be a great judge,' he had said in an interview.[10]

He said this as he felt that his father always had had a great sense of justice. 'My dad has a well-developed sense of justice,' he said. 'In fact, Washington as a state has one of the least-fair tax systems among all the states that puts extra burden on low-income residents.' Gates Sr. led a movement, '1098', that would have ensured greater fairness for all. He even volunteered for a bit role in a commercial for '1098' where he was dunked in a tank. 'He was about 78 or so, and I said, "Dad, what the heck!"' Although the movement failed, Gates Sr. was satisfied at being firm in his convictions.

Gates had always had high regard for his father's 'sense of judiciousness and collaborative spirit'. He feels that he did imbibe these qualities from his father but not in full measure as 'he has always been older than me,' he says in a lighter vein. 'He's very collaborative, very judicious, and he is serious about learning things and really knowing what he is talking about. He's good at stepping back and seeing the broad picture.' Gates's father passed away on Monday, 14 September 2020. The cause was Alzheimer's disease, his family said in an announcement on Tuesday. 'My dad was the "real" Bill Gates. He was everything I try to be and I will miss him every day,' Gates tweeted.

Given these qualities, both his parents, in an indirect way, did their bit in building Microsoft. One major area where Gates's parents did help in his initial years was to help many new employees 'feel at home'. Speaking of the time when many new people were brought in — many of them much older than Gates — he says, 'I figured out if they (his parents) were well older than me, they did a better job at connecting them into the community and whom they might want to know, and what groups they might like to be part of,' he said.

In addition to his parents, Gates has also mentioned his maternal grandmother and, later, his wife Melinda among the strong women who greatly influenced him in taking important decisions of his life. However, apart from the immediate family members, Gates has singled out one of his early teachers, Mrs Blanche Caffiere, a librarian in Seattle's View Ridge Elementary school, for special mention, as one who had had a major role to play in making him what he is today.

Mrs Blanche Caffiere

When Gates joined Seattle's View Ridge Elementary school, he was a typical young child, a little unsure of himself, and trying to find his place in the world. Somewhat embarrassed about his 'atrocious handwriting' and a 'comically messy desk', he would try to go unnoticed. At this point he was fortunate to find a kind support in Mrs Blanche Caffiere, school librarian and teacher. 'Mrs Caffiere took me under her wing and helped make it okay for me to be a messy, nerdy boy, who was fond of reading,' said Gates.

To probe and evoke his curiosity, she would often start with questions like, 'What do you like to read?' and 'What are you interested in?' She gave him great biographies she had read herself. She would genuinely listen to what he had to say. Gates recalls, 'Through those book conversations in the library and in the classroom, we became good friends.'[11]

Before she passed away in 2006, shortly after reaching her 100th birthday, Gates had an opportunity to thank her for the important role she had played in his life. He feels grateful to her for 'stoking my passion for learning' and, in a way, turning his life around.

PAUL ALLEN—THE PARTNER
WHO LEFT

When two equal partners are involved in a venture, a comparison is inevitable. At the same time, one needs to keep in mind that no two individuals are the same—they have their own pluses and minuses, strong and weak points. There's no doubt that in this comparison, Bill Gates certainly comes out stronger, scoring over Paul Allen. He was more dedicated to building his company, spent a greater amount of time at work and felt more involved in its day-to-day operation. But we can't ignore Paul Allen's role in laying the foundations of the company in its initial years—a fair analysis of his contribution can only be made by trying to understand his personality, and going deeper into his life story.

Paul Gardner Allen was born in Seattle on 21 January 1953, which made him almost three years older than Gates. Both his parents were librarians, his father being the associate director of the UW libraries. He also had a sister, Jody Allen, about six years younger than him. As his parents were academically inclined themselves, they were keen to see him do well at studies. They would be careful about his curriculum and his mother would get him a variety of reading material, junior science books and other texts to stimulate his interest in things around him. Their efforts paid off as he turned out to be bright student, getting a perfect score of 1600 in his SAT. We've already talked about his early days with Gates and while establishing Microsoft. Here, we'd like to refer to his contribution as a co-founder of Microsoft and where destiny took him after he left the company.

There's no doubt that Bill Gates remains the chief architect of Microsoft, but Paul Allen's role too cannot be undermined. We know that Allen made Gates's acquaintance sometime in 1968 when Gates had joined Lakeside School. Both were very inclined towards science and the concept of computer fascinated them. This common interest also became a bond between them. We must remind ourselves that at this stage, both were young boys with an age difference of about three years. During their formative years, children are not interested in terribly complicated analyses. When they parted company in 1983, they could look back at nearly 15 years of their association. At the time of severance, the two had had a frank discussion about their respective contributions in the business. But then, in a relationship, it becomes difficult to quantify many things—to work out a two-plus-two equation is not possible. In collaborations, human relationships, it's not just the question of professional or monetary support—there's an emotional and moral dimension to the whole process as well. A large number of fresh ventures start out on partnerships basis (Apple, HP, Google, Intel, etc.), as the co-founders need more emotional and moral support in the initial stages of building a business than later when the company is up and about and running well.

And so it was in this case too. Gates and Allen had been together for about 15 years, working, eating, smiling, laughing and also fighting together. There was much give-and-take on both sides. As we've mentioned before, in the school years Gates had been somewhat grateful to Allen for his companionship. He was also always ready to credit Allen for his vision, for his ability to think much ahead of his times. In the words of Bill Gates, Allen was 'immensely curious' and had very wide-ranging interests. 'He read more science fiction than I ever did. His office would be full of all kinds of magazines, though a little messy, represented his wide interests. He always wanted to find new and different things, always a little ahead of his time.'

If we look at their initial years, the success of Microsoft depended on basically two 'breakthrough' ventures: first, the BASIC programme for Altair, and then the O/S for the IBM-PC. At the time of their split, Gates had argued that he had done more work on BASIC, and to counter it, Allen said his contribution towards the O/S was more. Those could be called 'lovers' quarrels'. The reasons behind their split were much more fundamental. The two had had different personalities. While Gates was more focused on his venture, Allen had many other diverse interests. Besides computers, he was also interested in art, music, sports, travel, etc. While Gates was more of a hands-on manager, Allen was more of an outdoors man, and didn't quite like to be strait-jacketed into the limited duties of a manager. As a result, Gates would resort to pushing Allen, and according to Allen 'much more than he would be pushing others.' This would also result in 'screaming matches' between the two, sometimes running into hours.

So there came a breaking point, with the precipitating factor being Allen's illness.

New Entrepreneurial Dreams

In his earlier phase with Microsoft, Allen had had some experience of entrepreneurship. Now, with his new wealth and diverse interests he was able to explore new opportunities in the areas that interested him. After walking out of Microsoft, he set up Vulcan Inc. in 1986 with his sister Jody Allen as the controlling company for his investments in diverse fields.

With his resources, he was able to lay a roadmap for his future life. While on the one hand he made investments in fields that were close to his heart, on the other, he also used his money for philanthropic purposes and research in science and technology projects. His investments ranged from art, cable and film entertainment and the sciences to real estate and sports. As a result of his interest in sports, in 1988, he purchased the NBA team Portland Trail Blazers for $70 million and the NFL team Seattle Seahawks in 1996. Under his stewardship, the Seahawks made the Super Bowl thrice and won Super Bowl XLVIII. He was also involved in the design and construction of Century Link Field, an important stadium in Seattle. Ultimately, he went on to own seven important sports teams, fulfilling one of his dreams.

He had been a die-hard Jimi Hendrix fan. He pursued his music interest by joining bands and also played rhythm guitar in a Seattle band called Grown Man that released its first CD in the spring of 2000. Later, with his band Underthinkers, he released another album through Sony, *Everywhere at Once*. Much interested in the film and entertainment business, he made his Hollywood foray with substantial investments. Some of his noted productions here included films such as *Far from Heaven* (2002), *Hard Candy* (2005), *Where God left his Shoes* (2006), *Judgement Day: Intelligent Design on Trial* (2007), *This Emotional Life* (2010) and others. Many of his films even went on to get a lot of critical acclaim and win major international awards and nominations for Golden Globes and Academy Awards (such as *Far from Heaven*). An acclaimed production of his company was *Girl Rising*, a documentary that tells the stories of nine girls from nine countries who seek education. The background narrations of the film were done by major celebrities including Anne Hathaway, Cate Blanchett, Selena Gomez, Priyanka Chopra, Sushmita Sen and other international stars.

Travelling was always a passion, and to fulfill his dreams in this respect, Allen bought a luxury yacht, *Octopus*, which, at 414-ft long, happens to be one of the world's largest private yachts. In 2015, this yacht was also the site of his annual yacht party for Cannes Film Festival's Bollywood-themed party where the guests included Natalie Portman, Antonio Banderas, Leonardo Di Caprio and many other stars. Apart from personal use, travel and entertainment, Allen also often lent it out for exploratory and scientific ventures, and rescue missions. In 2002, he loaned the ship to the Royal British Navy to help it to retrieve the bell of the British battleship that had been sunk by the Germans in World War II. The historic bell was finally recovered with *Octopus*'s help in 2015, securing the yacht a place in history.

Art, music and cinema attracted Allen a great deal, but essentially, he was a man of science, and thus his interests in science and technology never waned. If Gates was a 'man of action', Allen has been called a 'man of ideas'. In addition to many soft projects, Allen also made forays into all kinds of science and tech ventures. His interests in aerospace moved him to fund the flight of SpaceShipOne, the first privately-funded effort to put a civilian in suborbital space. In its flight on 4 October 2004, it was able to climb to an altitude of 377,591 ft (10 times the flight height of commercial aircraft), and won the Ansari X prize of $10 million. In 2011, he launched another venture called Stratolaunch Systems with a view to launch satellites and eventually carry humans into space. Such projects, of course, take long to fully fructify. Allen passed away on 15 October 2018, but the company continued its operation with a Stratolaunch carrier aircraft making a maiden flight on 13 April 2019 and touching a height of 15,000 ft.

Besides many projects close to his heart, Allen also contributed towards a variety of philanthropic ventures that ranged from education, wildlife and environmental conservation to the arts and healthcare, community service and more. He was also the founder of Allen Institute for Brain Sciences, Institute for Artificial Intelligence and Institute for Cell Science. He had committed over $2 billion for such causes, making a positive impact in people's lives.

Since his exit from Microsoft, it had been a dream run for about 27 years. But then in 2009, he was diagnosed with Non-Hodgkin's lymphoma and needed to undergo treatment. At this point we'd like to clarify that though he had resigned from an active role in Microsoft, as he was a major shareholder, he continued to be on the board of directors. It was only on 9 November 2000 when he formally resigned from the Microsoft board of directors and accepted the position of senior strategy adviser to the company's executives. Over time, whatever bitterness Allen had felt at the time of leaving too had diminished by a great degree. During the 2009 illness, Gates visited Allen several times. Talking of Allen after his death, Gates said, 'Health had always been a major concern for him.' Gates felt that as his children have grown up, they could have connected more often and relived their past experiences. But that was not to be. In 2018, Allen again suffered a relapse of the earlier disease and died of septic shock on 15 October the same year.

Allen remained a lifelong bachelor. In some interviews, he spoke candidly about it, suggesting he was always open to romantic associations that might lead to marriage. In fact, in his early twenties, he did have a girlfriend, Rita, but at that time, he thought it to be too early to marry. That and his health apart, he didn't have too many regrets in life. Though born in a middle-class family, he was in many ways destiny's child making it to the top of the rich list of the world so early in life. Some of his investments and projects didn't go as planned because of management issues, and he saw his position slide among the richest. But then many others did work. *The Wall Street Journal* called Allen's South Lake Union real estate investment as 'unexpectedly lucrative' that made a $1.16 billion deal with Amazon.com in 2012. However, in 2014, he still had 100 million Microsoft shares, and at the time of his death in October 2018, he was the 44th richest man in the world with a net worth of $20.3 billion. Over time, he had received numerous awards and accolades, and was listed as among the 100 most influential men in the *Times* editions of 2007 and 2008. Despite setbacks, he had been able to lead a life above the ordinary and fulfill many of his dreams.

BARRIERS ON THE WAY

I n a marathon, it's too much to expect a smooth run all the way. Apart from the pressure of dealing with the competition and innovation, entrepreneurs' success stories are often marred by unexpected hurdles on the way. In the 1980s, Bill Gates and his team had been cruising along on a pleasant journey when they began to experience some unexpected jolts and bumps in their ride. First, the challenge of piracy and then the government's hard-nosed policies! The company was confident that these factors would not be able to affect their morale, but these issues were such that they called for attention and needed to be dealt with on a priority basis. Let's have a closer look at them separately.

Antitrust Case

In any society a conscientious government is supposed to play the role of a watchdog—an impartial arbiter—to ensure fair play between the competing entities! If, with money or tech power, an organization tries to curb others' right to grow or abuses its dominant status in any other way, it needs to be checked. This is the basis on which the US Sherman Antitrust Act was enacted by the US government in 1890. It was designed to 'protect trade and commerce against unlawful restraints and monopolies.' Over time, different sections of the law have been invoked against companies the government thought needed to be reined in. In the late 1960s, when the government thought that IBM was getting too big for comfort, they brought an antitrust case against the company, which dragged on for years. In fact, during this time in the post–World War II era, as the US emerged as the engine of growth, its companies and products were much in demand the world over. Some of them were becoming behemoths.

So, if it was IBM under the lens in the late 1960s, in the early '90s, it was the turn of Microsoft. It came to the notice of the authorities that because of its dominant position in the PC O/S market Microsoft had been misusing its power in pressurising its original equipment manufacturer (OEM) customers into coercive deals. In 1992, Federal Trade Commission began an independent fact-finding inquiry into the allegations. Initially, because nothing substantive could be established, the inquiry was closed on a tie, with two commissioners each voting for and against the move. The inquiry was closed in 1993. However, in the same year, on 21 May, US Attorney General Janet Reno took a suo moto cognizance of the case and began an inquiry on her own. In her inquiry, she found lapses and overstepping of the bounds of law by Microsoft. She also discovered that owing to its strong product in Windows O/S, the company had been taking unfair advantage of its position in the market.

Subsequently, in July 1994, the US Justice Department released a document detailing the terms and conditions of the agreement it had reached with Microsoft in this respect. It stated that between 1988 and 1994, Microsoft had abused its monopoly in the PC software market by compelling many OEMs to pay a royalty for each computer it sold containing a particular microprocessor, irrespective of whether the computer sold was with the

Microsoft O/S or with some other O/S. For example, if a company sold 100 computers but installed Windows on only 60, it had to pay the license fee for 100. This left PC manufacturers with only two options: either to stop using Windows and switch to the other product altogether or to comply with Microsoft's conditions. Since Windows ensured good sales, they couldn't afford to sever ties with Microsoft.

What followed was a kind of rap on the knuckles for Microsoft by the Justice Department. As there was some evidence of wrongdoing on the company's part, the authorities made Microsoft agree to certain conditions, whereby Microsoft would not compulsorily tie other products with the sale of Windows. The Justice Department's settlement with Microsoft stipulated that it would not compel its PC manufacturer clients on the following counts: forcing them to enter into processor-specific license contracts, purchasing any minimum number of O/S, entering into agreements of more than one year (though they could be renewed), paying the company on a lump sum basis, or purchasing other Microsoft products along with the Windows O/S.

However, this was not to be the end of the tunnel for Microsoft. Its real problems were to begin later. It was after the arrival of the Internet that the company was in for a major face-off with the government. In the beginning of the 1990s, the IT industry was poised for a big change with the arrival of the Internet. The Internet had introduced many new elements in the market that were to result in a major transformation of the industry and the general market on the whole. As the idea had begun to catch on, more and more servers were being linked together and a large number of files and data were being uploaded onto the Net. There came a pithy comment in this context: 'Internet is the biggest library in the world, but all the books are on the floor.' So, along with the growth of the Internet, there was also an immediate need for an efficient browser and even search engine that would help users access the data. Now it was a free-for-all to see who could produce a better browser and get ahead in the race.

Microsoft vs Netscape

The times were such that there was fierce competition in the air. The first major browser to hit the market was NCSA Mosaic that was released in September 1993. A graphical browser that was later ported to Apple

Macintosh and Windows, it displayed images in line with a document's text. It fired people's imagination and triggered a great deal of interest in the Internet. Marc Andreessen, who was the lead developer for Mosaic, later quit NCSA and formed his own company Netscape Communications Corporation. It released its flagship browser in October 1994 that was to take the market by storm and create serious issues with Microsoft. It was one of the drivers in the antitrust suit against the company. What followed had a major impact on the industry on the whole.

As far as the Internet was concerned, Microsoft had been a little slow to wake up to its reality. But then soon it began to play the catch-up game, and came out with its own browser, Internet Explorer, in August 1995. By the next year, compared to Netscape's 86 per cent share, Internet Explorer was able to get about 10 per cent on the whole. To increase its share, Microsoft adopted its typical time-tested strategy to piggyback its browser on the Windows O/S. It began to bundle IE with Windows, which meant it came free with Windows to the users. Since Windows was practically on very second PC, IE began to increase its market share exponentially. On the other hand, Netscape was a fine product, but unlike

Internet Explorer, had to be bought separately and took time to download, which was rather cumbersome. So, within four years of release while Internet Explorer's share had reached 75 per cent and by 1999, had gone up to 99 per cent, the others began to drop out of the picture. Microsoft was again ahead of the rest.

As things were heating up in the market, the involved parties couldn't be immune to its effects. In view of these developments, an antitrust suit was brought by the US Department of Justice and Attorney Generals of 20 US states against Microsoft for using monopoly practices to illegally thwart competition by using its software dominance. The case began on 18 May 1998. It was argued that the company had forced PC makers to install IE along with its Windows system. The DOJ was represented by David Boies. The case that lasted about one and a half years saw Bill Gates's testimonies and bitter arguments from both sides. A witness quoted a senior Microsoft employee as admitting to the company's intention to 'extinguish' and 'smother' rival Netscape and to 'cut off Netscape's air supply'. In support of the company's claims, Microsoft presented numerous videotapes, many of which were later found to be doctored. Gates was described as 'evasive and nonresponsive' by a source present in the court. He argued over the definitions of words like 'compete', 'concern', 'ask' and 'we'. He repeated the expression 'I don't recall' so many times that it even made the judge chuckle. Microsoft argued that the antitrust move against it was unfair and discriminatory in nature, and by constraining companies like itself, the government was simply playing in the hands of its inept and incompetent competitors, and in the process, curbing innovation and progress.

But considering all the aspects of the case, Microsoft was not on a very strong wicket. The judge Thomas Penfield Jackson ruled against them (in two parts) on 3 April 2000 indicting the company, and in June 2000, ordered a breakup of Microsoft as a 'remedy'. He ordered that the company be split into two parts: one to produce and manage the O/S and the other for software products. Microsoft appealed against the decision, and the D.C. Circuit Court of appeals overturned Judge Jackson's ruling against Microsoft, and later, on 6 September, the DOJ announced that it was not seeking the breakup of the company and would rather impose a lesser antitrust penalty. In follow-up of this, Microsoft agreed to settle with the contending parties on individual basis to address their various concerns.

These developments polarized the debate on the issue, with 240 leading economists writing an open letter to President Clinton, whereby they said that through many provisions of the Antitrust Act, the government was thwarting innovation and progress and should avoid playing in the hands of inept companies. On the other side, the critics of 'monopolistic practices' have continued to argue that companies such as Microsoft that become behemoths would remain difficult to control much to the detriment of general welfare. There's much to be said on both sides, and such issues involving many corporate giants continue to gain traction even in present times.

Piracy Woes

The lure of easy money would tempt anybody. And since piracy of 'intellectual rights' remains a rather low-risk crime, it attracts many. Not surprisingly, such trends have grown with the development of technology. In fact, piracy is the bane of any maker of a product that can be easily duplicated — music, video, film, book and now software (who could 'pirate' a car?). For the creator, it's a double whammy — loss of revenue, and a dampener for the talent — thus restricting future flowering of ideas. These were precisely the concerns that Bill Gates had raised at the beginning of his career, when he had designed his first major programme for Altair 8800. Although the product had been well received by computer enthusiasts, its popularity also proved to be a bane. Gates discovered that a pre-market copy had leaked into the community and was being copied and circulated in large numbers, which didn't bode well for software developers. He had always held that talent and creativity could never flourish without incentives and desired support of the concerned parties. Following this, in February 1976, he wrote an open letter to the hobbyists in MITS's in-house newsletter. He said, 'More than 90 per cent of users of MS Altair BASIC had not paid Microsoft. And by doing so, Altair hobby market was in the danger of eliminating incentive for any professional developers to produce, distribute and market high-quality software.' That was the beginning.

After the popularity of his MS-DOS, and later Windows, he was to face the real dimension of the problem. With PC offering a whole range of advantages, its demand had begun to rise not only in the US and the West, but also rest of the world. Since Windows was the O/S of choice, its growth too registered a steady increase. It was early days in 1993, when a trade journal in the US had reported that while the 'US has lost edge in the global manufacturing industry, it had gained in the computer software business.' Around this time, the US had over 80 per cent market share of the computer software in the world. But then the journal also pointed towards an accompanying problem. According to general estimates, the US was losing about $2 billion annually on account of software piracy in the US alone, and about five times in the rest of the world, which was increasing.

However, around this time, the world PC market was in a nascent stage. Over time, the problem could still be handled in the US and the West through better surveillance methods and law enforcement, but was to become more acute elsewhere. With the growth in the Chinese, Indian, South American and other markets of the world, it was set to assume alarming proportions. Interestingly, in 2004, on a visit to China, Bill Gates was asked by a senior government official about Microsoft's income from China. When he mentioned a figure, the official was surprised and he asked the interpreter to double check with Gates. The official thought the figure should have been sufficiently higher given the demand for computers in China. But the figure was correct, as software piracy was rampant in the country and only a very small percentage of computers ran on genuine software.

While on the one hand, China was a big market for Microsoft, on the other, it was also losing a lot of revenue due to the menace of piracy. In an interview in November 2018, Steve Ballmer told *Fox News* that when he left Microsoft a few years earlier, 90 per cent of Chinese companies were using Windows, and in China alone, Microsoft was losing upwards of $10 billion annually due to piracy. Even in India, another large market for Microsoft, the problem has been rather serious. As of 2021, pirated Windows software is available for a few hundred rupees, while the original software's cost is in the thousands. The reality check is, while large corporations, on account of visibility and transparency, cannot afford to risk pirated software, individuals and small businesses escape the radar of surveillance and save on the expensive programme. In fact, in India, very often the hardware vendor himself would offer a free

Windows copy along with computer to boost his sale and retain the competitive edge. Customers would like to save money wherever they can.

Microsoft has attempted to deal with the issue in a variety of ways—online checks, offers of incentives, cost cutting and even physical action with the support of local law enforcement agencies. In 2009, the company launched its 'Windows Genuine Advantage' programme, where it informed the user about the benefits of using genuine software, outlined how it would provide better security and performance with regular updates. Despite the increase in the problem, it had become possible for the Microsoft team to detect counterfeit software by locating the IP address. In such cases, the background screen of the computer would turn black. The company would send an automated message to the users, 'You could be a victim of counterfeit software' and also urged them to procure genuine software, and enjoy benefits like updates and tech support.

Microsoft had felt greatly encouraged by the support extended to its efforts by a lot of countries. In 2000, it was able to take legal action against piracy and illegal counterfeiting in 22 countries with the help of local authorities. In countries that ranged from Argentina,

Brazil, Canada, Columbia, Germany, Hong Kong and Peru to Poland, Philippines, China, Romania, the US and the UK, operations were carried on a sustained basis. It was reported in 2001 that over five million units of illegal software and hardware products of Microsoft were seized worldwide in the previous year. In 2009, Mexican authorities conducted a massive raid with about 300 guards on an illegal operation in Los Reyes, a town in Mexico. Three arrests were made in the operation for duplicating Microsoft CDs, MS Office software and Xbox video games. Over 50 duplicating machines were also seized. In India, too, there have been a number of raids by authorities from time to time at the offices of some companies suspected of using counterfeit products. The efforts have yielded results.

However, since China has been an important market for Microsoft, the company adopted some country-specific measures here. It drastically reduced the price to deter users from opting for the pirated copies. Lenovo is China's largest PC manufacturer with 36.7 per cent market share. It used to ship bare computers, sans O/S. In 2013, Microsoft was able to persuade the company to sell hardware with pre-installed software. In a counter-point, some industry commentators have argued that

Microsoft is not too serious about combating the piracy problem as it had a contribution in making Bill Gates the richest person in the world. They say that easy and 'almost free' availability of Windows software made a whole new generation of young people part of the Windows ecosystem, who later formed part of the workforce and preferred the Windows systems at their offices. They felt at home using the Windows O/S and it acted as a catalyst in giving a boost to the sale of Windows.

Windows has been an original O/S for a variety of PC brands. But it needed to take the competition in its stride. One of the main contenders since the mid-1990s, Linux, is an open-source software and thus free. Unlike Windows, it can be downloaded by any user, who could make his own alterations and modifications and use it. But it involves a greater degree of effort on the user's part and has been more suited for server applications and professionals. The main and distinct advantage of the Windows O/S has been its user-friendly features, making it extremely easy to use even for a beginner with no previous computer experience. So, it was contented that while the pirated Windows had been easily available and 'almost free', why would a common user opt for Linux? Although free, Linux suited professionals more than the general user. So, did piracy, in an indirect, way help to make Microsoft so big? Did Microsoft turn a blind eye to piracy and deliberately went easy on it? The jury is still out.

THE SUCCESSORS

Although the names Microsoft and Bill Gates are almost synonymous even today, we need to remind ourselves that it's been 20 years since Gates stepped down as the CEO of the company and made way for his old associate and friend Steve Ballmer. Fourteen years later, in 2014, Ballmer gave up the position, with Satya Nadella taking over as the chief. Thus, to fully comprehend the success and growth story of Microsoft, we also need to look at the contributions of both the successors.

Steve Ballmer

Stephen Anthony Ballmer was born on 24 March 1956 in Detroit in a well-to-do Michigan family. His father

Fredric Henry Ballmer was a Swiss immigrant and a manager at the Ford Motor Company, and mother, Beatrice Dworkin, was an American Belarusian Jew whose family traced its origins to Iran. Even as a child, Steve showed a lot of promise—so much so that when he was eight, his father had declared that one day his son would make it to Harvard. And so he did! He excelled in academics, and when he graduated from his preparatory school in Michigan, he had a score of 800 on the mathematical section of SAT and was a National Merit scholar. He joined Harvard in 1973 and lived down the hall from his college-mate Bill Gates. Their acquaintance here was to turn into a lifelong association with much give and take on both sides.

Ballmer graduated *magna cum laude* (an honour indicating the distinction with which the degree has been earned) from Harvard in 1977 with a bachelor's in applied mathematics and economics. After briefly trying his hand at writing screenplays in Hollywood and dropping out of Stanford Graduate School of Business, he joined Microsoft on 11 June, 1980 as the 30th employee of the company and the first manager to be hired by Bill Gates. With a handsome salary and an offer of shares, Ballmer owned 8 per cent of the company when it was incorporated in 1981.

He took over as CEO on 11 June 2000, and was succeeded by Satya Nadella on 4 February 2014. His 14-year tenure at the company has been reviewed with mixed reactions. On the whole, it can be rated as above par. During his time, Microsoft's annual turnover increased from $25 billion to $70 billion, and the net income increased by 215 per cent to $23 billion. Annual profit growth at 16.4 per cent was much better than that achieved by Jack Welch of GE and IBM's Louis V. Gerstner Jr. However, due to the lackluster performance of Microsoft's stock price during his time, he has been criticized by many an industry watcher. Adam Hartung of the *Forbes* magazine called him 'the worst CEO of a large publicly traded American company.' And David Einhorn, a major hedge fund manager, said that Ballmer's continued presence was the 'biggest overhang on Microsoft's stock'. Following this sentiment, when Ballmer resigned in 2014, the Microsoft share suddenly jumped up on the news.

We can say that these critics have been rather harsh on him. First of all, he took over at the height of the market bubble. The market needed time to revive, and he needed a lot of resilience to keep his head above water. Moreover, when he took over in 2000, the industry had turned a corner. Microsoft's flagship products, Windows and other applications had been firmly established in the market. In view of this, he went about restructuring the company and replacing many division heads. He felt that the company had had enough of the software push, and it was time for a substantial hardware exposure. His tenure saw several major changes, with emphasis on many new concepts. He built a number of new divisions. Data Centre Division, Xbox Entertainment and Devices Division and Enterprise Business were his initiatives that paid rich dividends for the company in coming time.

Ballmer thought that as there wasn't much threat to company's software products, activities could be expanded to include diverse hardware areas too. The first installment of Xbox series of consoles was released in 2001. Azure, the company's foray into cloud computing, was announced as 'Project Red Dog' in 2008 and released on 1 February 2010 as Windows Azure (before being named Microsoft Azure on 25 March 2014). The first retail Microsoft Store opened on 22 October 2009 in Scottsdale Arizona. Surface, the first computer (tablet) with Microsoft's own hardware, was unveiled on 18 June 2012 and launched the same year on 26 October. And then on 3 September 2013, the company announced the decision to buy Nokia's mobile phone unit, and acquired it on 25 April 2014 for $7.2 billion. Earlier, on 4 February 2014, Ballmer had stepped down as the CEO with the India-born Satya Nadella taking over from him. On the same day, John W. Thompson took over as the chairman and it was announced that Bill Gates would continue to be associated with the company in the role of technology adviser. In fact, in 2008, around the time of Gates's exit, Ballmer had announced that he intended to stay on in Microsoft for a decade more, but perhaps the general environment and criticism of his performance made him revise his decision.

A fair assessment of his tenure would indicate that all through his stay, he did work on a sound strategy. Although he worked on expansion, he didn't let go of the company's grip on the cash-cow products like Windows and Office applications. He worked to ward off whatever threats would come therein. Some commentators have remarked that he killed innovation at the cost of perpetuating Windows and Office products. In fact, his period saw a very strategic upgradation of its Office products. Some of the most successful Windows versions were released during his tenure. Windows XP was released for retail sale on 25 October 2001, Windows 7 came into the market on 22 October 2009, and although Windows 10 was released on 29 July 2015, work on it had begun much earlier, during his period.

A colourful exuberant personality, Steve Ballmer has also been known for his abrasive and assertive style of functioning. Although shy as a child, he later turned out to be an aggressive executive, often hyperventilating his feelings at the time of stress or on special occasions. Despite the fact that he had been rather close to Gates for a long time, it has been reported that there was tension surrounding the transition of authority. According to sources, on one occasion, there was much screaming and shouting over Ballmer defending some employees, with Gates leaving the meeting in a huff. During the antitrust case he could not hold back his feelings against Attorney General Janet Reno. 'How many of you think... the kind of integration in this product actually will be good for you?' he asked the audience in a conference. On approval from the audience, he said, 'Then I say the heck with Janet Reno at this point.' In July 2000, piqued over Linux eating into the Windows share, he described it as 'communism'. Earlier in June, he had called Linux a 'cancer that attaches itself in an intellectual property sense to everything it touches.' Mark Lucovsky, who left the company in 2004, testified in a Washington State Court that upon hearing that he had planned to quit the company for Google, 'Ballmer picked up a chair and threw it across the room hitting a table in his office.'

On happier occasions, he could also be seen in company's promotion commercials prancing about and making excessive use of his lung power. On the event of celebration of the 25th anniversary of Microsoft in September 2000, he jumped across the stage shouting, 'I love this company' — the jig was later nicknamed as 'monkey boy dance.' In another video filmed on the Windows 2000 Developers' Conference he can be seen perspiring and chanting, 'Developers, Developers.' As we've mentioned earlier, this tendency also had had negative fallout, and at one time, he needed to have surgery on his throat.

At the time of him joining Microsoft in 1980, Steve Ballmer was offered 5–10 per cent of the company. In 1981, when Microsoft was incorporated, he owned 8 per cent of the company shares, and with stock options offered over the years, he has become one of the richest persons in the world. As of October 2019, he was the sixteenth richest person in the world with a personal wealth of $51.9 billion. Post retirement, to keep himself occupied, he acquired Los Angeles Clippers of the National Basketball Association (NBA), much like another old Microsoft hand, Paul Allen, who also went in for sports teams. In 1990, he married Connie Snyder and the couple has three sons.

Satya Nadella

Although Steve Ballmer had declared in 2008 that he planned to remain the CEO for another 10 years, he threw in the towel in 2014, apparently upset by some of the setbacks the company suffered and general criticism of his performance. The choice for the successor finally zeroed in on to the India-born Satya Nadella, who had been with the company since 1992 and had proved his mettle in various positions and departments.

Satya Narayana Nadella was born on 19 August 1967 in Hyderabad, India, and attended a public school in the city. His father was a member of the Indian Administrative Service, Government of India.

After graduating in Electrical Engineering from Manipal Institute of Technology, Karnataka, he got an MS in Computer Science from the University of Wisconsin-Milwaukee and an MBA from Booth School of Business, University of Chicago. Having worked in Sun Microsystems for some time, he joined Microsoft in 1992. At Microsoft, he worked in various positions and was the president of the company's Server and Tool Business before becoming the chief in 2014.

On the whole, his performance in last five years has been rated as above par by the analysts. Microsoft's share value had tripled by September 2018 with a growth of 27 per cent on an annual basis. When he took over, he had been rather conscious of the lackluster performance of the company's share. At this juncture, what helped him was the unchallenged position of Windows in certain areas and his experience in cloud-related technologies. Before taking over as the chief, as the president of the Server and Tools Business, he had been able to initiate many positive changes and brought database, Windows Server and developer tools to the cloud operation. As a consequence, the revenue from the cloud grew to $20.3 billion in June 2013 from 16.6 billion when he took over in 2011.

Now, as the chief, he could go full-steam ahead in initiating the changes he desired. After taking over, he got rid of a lot of dead wood in the company and made the operation leaner and meaner. Many mid-level managers were fired. He was able to put the company on a strong footing on account of a slew of new measures. While the Bill Gates-era vision statement was a 'PC on every desk and in every home, running Microsoft software,' Nadella went for a change in the company's philosophy with the goal to 'empower every person and every organization on the planet to achieve more.' He felt it was time to engage with other competitors rather than being hostile to them. This also meant a greater openness and a spirit of cooperation rather than confrontation with the companies Microsoft is at loggerheads with, such as Apple, IBM, Google and Amazon. Microsoft also joined the Linux Foundation as a platinum member. He has also supervised a number of strategic acquisitions like Mojang, a Swedish game company, for $2.5 billion in 2014, Xamarin and LinkedIn in 2016 and GitHub in 2018. A few months after joining, he briefly courted controversy when he said that women should not ask for a raise and trust the system. After criticism, he retracted his statement. Under his stewardship the company seems to be heading towards wider and brighter horizons.

In 1992, Nadella married Anupama, who's the daughter of his father's batchmate in the Indian Administrative Service. His junior at Manipal University, she was pursuing her Bachelor's in Architecture at the time. The couple has three children, a son and two daughters. His net worth is estimated at $250 million.

AN EYE ON THE FUTURE

Which is the largest computer company in the world? If we look around, we see five to six names with whom we normally interact on a regular basis or whose products we use. If Apple is the big boy of smartphones, IBM leads in large computers and mainframes. If Amazon is a forerunner in e-tailing, Google is the Internet giant. If Facebook commands a large share in social media, Microsoft has the software on which the world is running today.

Since our subject here is Microsoft, we would like to assess its position vis-à-vis its competitors and see where the company is headed in future. The IT industry has been characterized by a high degree of fluidity—with constant innovation and fast obsolescence being a running theme. As a result, it's difficult to assign a particular position to any specific company. However, in terms of value, Apple, Amazon, Alphabet, Facebook and Microsoft have been competing with one another, with their value steadily on the rise. According to recent reports, the market capitalization of Apple, Inc. had crossed $2 trillion and that of Microsoft had gone up to $1.765 trillion. These figures of course rise and fall depending on the success and failure of a particular product and its resultant effect on the company's stock price.

Today, Microsoft is in direct competition with Apple in the hardware business such as PCs and tablets, with companies like Oracle and Red Hat (acquired by IBM in July 2019) in software and enterprise business, with Amazon, Google and IBM in web services and cloud computing, with Sony and Nintendo in gaming gadgets and with Google in search engines. One major advantage Microsoft enjoys is that it has the widest spread of the net in computer-related products. It features in almost all the segments while others are heavily dependent on some specific products. For instance, in the case of Apple, Inc., a January 2021 report by Statista Research Department shows 44.26 per cent of its revenue in third quarter of 2020 came from the sales of the iPhones and ever since the demise of its visionary leader, Steve Jobs, the company has been unable to come out with any breakthrough product.

Undoubtedly, among all the IT majors today, Microsoft is perhaps the most product-diversified company. Its reach is broad and product range wide. True, in the earlier times, it too suffered from a heavy, product-specific focus and was particularly dependent on Windows and Office revenues. But with Steve Ballmer gradually diversifying into other areas like gaming, hardware and cloud computing, and later Satya Nadella building and consolidating on them, the company today is sitting pretty as far its business operations and revenues are concerned.

Keeping in tune with the changing times, in July 2013, Microsoft had decided to reorganize its business under new divisions. It constituted four new business divisions under which all the operations were re-organized, namely, operating systems, apps, cloud and devices. All previous divisions were dissolved without any layoffs. Subsequently, more restructuring was undertaken.

Currently, the business has been organized under three main heads:

1. Intelligent Cloud
2. Productivity and Business Processes
3. More Personal Computing

Microsoft's revenue in the financial year ended 2020 was $143.015 billion. On the whole, the performance has been generally above expectations, with the three operating groups recording a rise in revenue over the previous year: Intelligent Cloud improving by 24 per cent at $48.36 billion; Productivity and Business Processes recording 13 per cent growth at $46.39 billion; and More Personal Computing registering 6 per cent rise at $48.25 billion. According to observers, while earlier Windows and Office and their related products and services had had a greater share in company's total revenues, in the near future, cloud operation is slated to overtake it.

The company has been working towards its two-fold objective: to continue to consolidate on its established products while making increasing thrust on the technologies of future. E-tailing, social media, cloud computing and AI have been among the major current technologies which would go a long time into future too. Further, enterprise business would always be a major revenue earner for the IT companies. However, from Microsoft's point of view, its increasing emphasis has now been on cloud computing and AI apart from its other businesses.

Cloud Computing

As indicated by the 2020 revenue figures, Microsoft's cloud computing business has been a bright spot on its balance sheet, offsetting its earlier heavy dependence on Windows. The company continues to make aggressive forays in this area. In October 2019, in a competitive bid for the project called JEDI (Joint Enterprise Defense Infrastructure), Microsoft beat rivals such as Amazon, Oracle and IBM to be awarded a $10 billion cloud contract by the US Department of Defense.[12] Despite Amazon's objection to the award to Microsoft and subsequent legal filings, on 4 September 2020, the Department of Defense reaffirmed that Microsoft had won the award, and their proposal 'continues to be the best value to the government.' In its 17 February 2020 report, *The Asian Age*, quoting Garner Consulting, stated that worldwide, the general cloud business in the year 2020 was expected to reach $266 billion, recording an increase of 17 per cent over the previous year.

Since the concept of cloud computing is comparatively new, it would be helpful at this juncture to understand it in a more comprehensive manner. In the early days of the Internet, a lot of people would remark that email comprised 80 per cent of their web usage. In time, it dawned on people that when you could send letters and pictures through email, why not larger files and data? And thus was born the idea of cloud computing, which began to take concrete shape with Amazon releasing Elastic Compute Cloud in 2006. As the idea caught on, Microsoft began working on it as it has been detailed earlier in the book. Windows Azure was formally launched in February 2010, and it was later named Microsoft Azure on 25 March 2014.

However, fortunately for Microsoft, in addition to Windows, the company has been able to make its mark in new technology areas like cloud computing, Azure Service platform and gaming consoles business. The company has continued to explore newer avenues and expand in other areas. Through a project named 'Azure Government', it has partnered with 17 American intelligence agencies to develop products that track American citizens. It has also developed special equipment for the army called Microsoft HoloLens headsets that enhance the troops' capabilities to engage with the enemy using high-power detection of the troops' movement.

The concept has been catching on as it offers a few never-before-seen advantages for big establishments. With this facility, companies no longer need to host expensive servers at their premises which saves costs, and moreover, data is accessible even when one is on the move over the Internet. Additionally, the facility offers many other value-added advantages earlier not available with on-site equipment. Today, the services offered by Microsoft include serverless computing, virtual machine scale sets, service fabric for micro services and container orchestration, virtual and content delivery networks to traffic managers, file and disc storage, Azure-developed Test Labs, site recovery, container registry, SQL-based databases and related tools, stream analytics, tools for developing artificial capabilities, variety of machine learning, security centre, visual studio team services, resource manager, log analytics and automation, besides many other services.

Microsoft's deep thrust in the area has earned it an enviable position among the top vendors (and contenders) in the field, as a 'highly reliable and secure public Cloud provider'. One of the main reasons for it to surge ahead of competition is the fact that a large number of networks around the globe are Windows backed. And since Azure offers a kind of seamless connectivity, it's the service of choice. Above all, it offers a vibrant ecosystem, by having collaborative arrangements with many other computer companies like Red Hat, HPE, Adobe, Cisco and others.

Its major clients include government institutions as it has been able to highlight 'its security and compliance capabilities', with its website claiming that Azure has been recognized 'as the most trusted cloud for US government institutions, including a FedRAMP high authorization that covers 118 Azure services.' With an aggressive player like Microsoft in the arena, the cloud wars seem to be heating up. No wonder, Azure has begun to play catch up with the pioneer AWS. According to a February 2021 statista.com report, Amazon's revenue from AWS was $45.37 billion as against Microsoft's Intelligent Cloud revenue of $48.36. And with the prestigious Pentagon contract, Microsoft has stolen an impressive march over other rivals. Although IBM had been an early entrant on the scene, it eventually lagged behind. To make up for this, it acquired Red Hat for $34 billion in October 2018. It's been an expensive acquisition but IBM hopes to improve its annual balance sheet by over $3 billion or even more in coming future.

Artificial Intelligence

Another important technology area that has been on everyone's mind is AI. Although the concept is old, it's only in recent times with advances in related areas that it has started getting traction. With AI becoming one of the frontline sciences of recent times, large investments are being made in it. There are factories in advanced countries where a large quantum of work is handled by robots, with robotics being an academic discipline in universities and engineering institutes.

Concrete progress in this direction was only made possible with the development of computers. Scientists had begun to wonder that when computers could perform increasingly complex functions, why not independent thinking? And thus was born the concept of AI. Work on it had begun in earnest at the Dartmouth College in 1956. Scientists and engineers from some of the leading facilities such as MIT, CMU and IBM had begun working on such projects, and in a few years, were able to report significant progress. Observers and the press called some of their achievements 'astonishing'. It was found that the computers had been beating even humans in some standard tasks like solving mathematical problems. Even when pitted against humans in some common board games like Checkers, computers were found to be scoring better.

Such breakthroughs had set the US Defense Department thinking about its utility in creating new devices of defence and offence, and following this, the government increased funding and laboratories were set up all over the world. Herbert Alexander Simon, a leading economist and cognitive scientist had declared around that time, 'machines will be capable, within 20 years of doing any work a man can do.'[13] Another leading authority in AI, Marvin Minsky agreed with him and said, 'Within a generation ... the problem of creating Artificial Intelligence will substantially be solved.' However, the confidence these proponents of the discipline exuded at that time gradually began to wane as unexpected problems and hurdles cropped up. As the government cut funding, a long AI winter set in the field which could only thaw with fresh advancements in the future.

Since the technology held tremendous potential, new research began in this area again in the eighties. The success of Expert System (a machine that emulates the human decision-making process), and the launch of Japanese Fifth Generation Computer Systems, revived new interest in AI. Although the AI market had reached over a billion US dollars in 1985, some reverses again slowed progress here. But by now, IT had become unstoppable, and in the late nineties, the development of more powerful computers and advances in other fields gave a major push to the technology. At present, we have robot-driven manufacturing facilities around the globe and intelligent machines like Siri, Alexa and Google Home in our households. Despite robot-driven cars and remote controlling of household appliances fast becoming a reality, it is still early days to gauge what the future holds for AI.

Overall, one reason for Microsoft's success has been its practice to be alert and agile in engaging with the prevailing market trends. It had begun to make early investments in AI because of this tendency and continued to show deeper interest in it as time passed.

One of its first major projects in this field was Kinetic, which used motion-sensing inputs to help user control and interact with the gaming consoles Xbox One and Xbox 360. Using the webcam as an accessory to aid in operation and without the gaming controller, the player would use just gestures and spoken commands to play the game. The objective was to enhance the user experience with this value-added feature.

Gaming devices continued to be extremely popular with video game players, with new innovations being introduced in them regularly. Though the Kinetic inputs didn't find much traction with players, the technology had positive result in other areas. Its low-cost advanced features have found their use in many other fields including Microsoft's cloud computing platform Azure. Another major development in this field has been the use of simultaneous language translation on Skype. Skype, the telecommunication application, that facilitates communication over the Internet had been acquired by Microsoft in 2010. Now, with its AI features, simultaneous translation of many languages including English, French, German, Chinese, Italian, Spanish and others has been made available to the user, expanding its reach and scope.

As far as Microsoft is concerned, AI activities on their own may not be producing perceptible revenue to impact the company's books, but investments in research have been leading to accruing of advantages in other areas. Its indirect role is perceptible in every area of operation to improve its performance and productivity. Given its utility in diverse spheres of human activity in coming time, AI has been rated as the defining technology of our times. Aware of its growing importance, Microsoft set up its Artificial Intelligence and Research Group with 5,000 computer scientists and engineers in 2016. The group has been making AI contributions in different areas, ranging from building language translators, making gaming consoles, improving machine learning, examining the societal and individual impact of the spread of intelligent technologies and developing interactive tools (like Word Writer) and innovative platforms for cyber physical systems and robotics, besides other fields.

Given all these trends and Microsoft's involvement in them, the outlook of the company undoubtedly appears to be bright. Since 2014, when Nadella took over Microsoft's operations, the stock price of the company has been doing well in the market. On 24

February 2021, it was US $230 per share as against $174 on 25 February 2020, having appreciated over 30 per cent in last year alone, after nine splits (bonuses) since its IPO in 1986. As of 25 January 2021, Bill Gates was the third richest man in the world with a net worth of $132 billion (with Elon Musk at $197 billion and Jeff Bezos $182 billion) testifying to his faith in the company he founded. Individual fortunes of the founders however may go up or down with time, but their enormous contributions to humankind would always be valued.

EPILOGUE

Since its humble beginning in a garage in Albuquerque, New Mexico, Microsoft has indeed come a long way through the decades. Bill Gates had indicated earlier on that if revolution had to happen, they better be part of it. At the time, none of the players involved in it had any idea how the whole IT movement would play out in the long run and what role their company would play in it. The way Microsoft has emerged as a colossus on the technology landscape is a matter of pride for all those involved in making it what it is. Microsoft's contribution in shaping modern history is significant indeed. It has left its imprint on every other activity humanity is involved in.

However, the future is another story. In a fast changing and evolving world, growth and progress are anyone's game. But despite challenges, Microsoft appears to be all geared up to script another chapter in its long history of impressive achievements. Its past and present point towards a brighter tomorrow.

REFERENCE

1   Gates, William H. and Collins Hemingway. *Business @ the Speed of Thought: Succeeding in the Digital Economy.* Penguin, 1999.
2   'Intel Now Packs 100 Million Transistors in Each Square Millimeter.' *IEEE Spectrum: Technology, Engineering, and Science News,* spectrum.ieee.org/nanoclast/ semiconductors/processors/intel-now-packs-100-million-transistors-in-each-square-millimeter. Accessed on 20 January 2021.
3   Cringely, Robert X. 'Part II'. *Triumph of the Nerds: The Rise of Accidental Empires.* Season 1. PBS, June 1996. Archived from the original on 13 August 2017. Accessed on 20 January 2021.
4   '"This Week" Transcript: Michele Bachmann and Bill Gates.' *ABC News Network,* abcnews.go.com/Politics/ week-transcript-michele-bachmann-Gates-gates/ story?id=14845751. Accessed on 20 January 2021.
5   Caruso, Denise. 'Company Strategies Boomerang.' *InfoWorld,* 2 April 1984.

6   Gates, Bill, and Janet Lowe. *Bill Gates Speaks: Insight from the World's Greatest Entrepreneur*. John Wiley & Sons, Inc., 1998.

7   'Paul Allen and the Birth of the PC, Microsoft.' *CBS News*, CBS Interactive, www.cbsnews.com/news/Allen-allen-and-the-birth-of-the-pc-microsoft-2011-60-minutes-interview/. Accessed on 20 January 2021.

8   Isaacson, Walter. *Steve Jobs: A Biography*. Simon & Schuster, 2011.

9   'TRANSCRIPT–Bill Gates and Steve Jobs at D5.' *AllThingsD*, allthingsd.com/20070531/d5-gates-jobs-transcript/. Accessed on 20 January 2021.

10   Stiffler, Lisa. 'Interview: Bill Gates Talks about His Dad's Influence on His Life, the Tech Community and the World.' *GeekWire*, 30 November 2015, www.geekwire.com/2015/qa-ish-with-Gates-gates-jr/. Accessed on 20 January 2021.

11   Gates, Bill. 'A Teacher Who Changed My Life.' *Gatesnotes. com*, www.gatesnotes.com/Education/A-Teacher-Who-Changed-My-Life. Accessed on 20 January 2021.

12   'Microsoft Beats Amazon for Pentagon's USD 10 Billion Cloud Computing Contract.' *The Asian Age*, 28 October 2019, www.asianage.com/technology/in-other-news/281019/microsoft-beats-amazon-for-pentagons-usd-10-Billion-cloud-computing-contract.html. Accessed on 20 January 2021.

13   Press, Gil. 'A Very Short History of Artificial Intelligence (AI).' *Forbes*, 30 December 2016, www.forbes.com/sites/gilpress/2016/12/30/a-very-short-history-of-artificial-intelligence-ai/?sh=5630ddca6fba. Accessed on 20 January 2021.

BIBLIOGRAPHY

'A Brief History of Anti-Piracy at Microsoft.' *ZDNet*, www.zdnet.com/article/a-brief-history-of-anti-piracy-at-microsoft/. Accessed on 22 October 2020.

'A Brief History of Microsoft—The World's Biggest Software Company.' *DSP Blog*, content.dsp.co.uk/a-brief-history-of-microsoft-the-worlds-biggest-software-company. Accessed on 28 November 2020.

'Adobe Ready with Next Gen Creative Cloud.' *The Times of India*, New Delhi. 5 November 2019.

'AI Courses a Bigger Draw for Experienced Techies.' *The Times of India*, New Delhi. 21 June 2019.

'AI Has Become So Simple and Affordable That Anyone Can Use It.' *The Times of India*, New Delhi. 18 June 2019.

'Allen Sues Google, Apple, Others over Patents.' *Reuters*. 28 August 2010.

'Amplifying Human Ingenuity with Microsoft AI.' *Cloud Computing Services*, azure.microsoft.com/en-us/resources/videos/build-2018-amplifying-human-ingenuity-with-microsoft-ai/. Accessed on 18 October 2020.

'Apple Services Revenue Hits All-Time High.' *The Times of India*, New Delhi. 5 November 2019.

'Australian Prime Minister Says Bing Could Replace Google.' *The Economic Times*, 1 February 2021.

'Bill Gates Breaks Down 6 Moments from His Life.' *Wired*, 17 October 2018, www.youtube.com/watch?v=GzUUghxDhYM. Accessed on 26 October 2020.

'Bill Gates—I Helped Steve Jobs Create the Mac.' *Computerworld*, 31 October 2011, www.computerworld.com/article/2471512/bill-gates----i-helped-steve-jobs-create-the-mac.html. Accessed on 24 December 2020.

'Bill Gates Tops Jeff Bezos as World's Richest.' *The Times of India*, New Delhi. 17 November 2019.

'From Windows 1 to Windows 10: 29 Years of Windows Evolution.' *The Guardian*, 2 October 2014, www.theguardian.com/technology/2014/oct/02/from-windows-1-to-windows-10-29-years-of-windows-evolution. Accessed on 29 October 2020.

'History and Evolution of Microsoft Office Software.' *The Windows Club*, 24 January 2021, www.thewindowsclub.com/history-evolution-microsoft-office-software. Accessed on 6 November 2020.

'History of Computing.' *Encyclopædia Britannica*, www.britannica.com/technology/computer/History-of-computing. Accessed on 2 October 2020.

'It's Official: Big Tech to Face All-Round Antitrust Probe.' *The Times of India*, New Delhi. 5 June 2019.

'Lifelike Robots That Can Learn, Adapt May Be a Reality Soon.' *The Asian Age*, New Delhi. 25 August 2019.

'Mary Maxwell Gates.' *NNDB*, www.nndb.com/people/602/000122236/. Accessed on 17 January 2021.

'Microprocessor History: Architecture & Its Generations.' *ElProCus*, 9 February 2021, www.elprocus.com/microprocessor-history-and-brief-information-about-its-generations/. Accessed on 1 November 2020.

'Microsoft Backs Search Engines Paying for News Worldwide.' *Mint*, 12 February 2021.

'Microsoft Confirms Takeover of Skype.' *BBC News*, 10 May 2011, www.bbc.com/news/business-13343600. Accessed on 8 October 2020.

'Microsoft Corporation.' *Encyclopædia Britannica*, www.britannica.com/topic/Microsoft-Corporation. Accessed on 27 November 2020.

'Microsoft India Revenue Hits $1 Billion for First Time.' *The Times of India*, New Delhi. 24 October 2019.

'Microsoft Offers to Step in if Rival Google Quits Australia.' *The Economic Times*, 3 February 2021.

'Microsoft Partners with Social Alpha to Boost Healthtech Startups in India.' *Mint*, 19 November 2020.

'Microsoft Redesigns Excel with Custom Live Data Types — Key Features and More.' *Mint*, 30 October 2020.

'Microsoft Sharpens Focus on Hybrid Cloud with Azure Stack HC!' *Mint*, 21 September 2020.

'Microsoft Word.' *Encyclopædia Britannica*, www.britannica.com/technology/Microsoft-Word. Accessed on 6 October 2020.

'MS, Intel May Have Fallen Out.' *The Asian Age*, New Delhi. 27 June 2019.

'MS Interested in xCloud Exclusives.' *The Asian Age*, New Delhi. 25 November 2019.

'MS Teases Dual-screen Surface Device.' *The Asian Age*, New Delhi. 7 June 2019.

'MS Teases Next-Gen XBOX, "Scarlet", Microsoft Set to Unveil Specifications of Its Next-Generation Xbox Console at Its Event E3 at Los Angeles.' *The Asian Age*, New Delhi. 10 June 2019.

'MS Warns Users About Malware.' *The Asian Age*, New Delhi. 26 June 2019.

'Office Romance: How Bill Met Melinda.' *The Independent*, 23 October 2011, www.independent.co.uk/life-style/gadgets-and-tech/features/office-romance-how-bill-met-melinda-855292.html. Accessed on 3 January 2021.

'Operating System Market Share Worldwide.' *StatCounter Global Stats*, gs.statcounter.com/os-market-share. Accessed on 28 December 2020.

'Paul Allen on Gates, Microsoft.' *YouTube*, CBS 60 Minutes, www.youtube.com/watch?v=4IM0SvIiMI4. Accessed on 5 January 2021.

'Pentagon Snubs Amazon, Gives Microsoft $ 10 Billion Deal.' *The Asian Age*, New Delhi. 27 October 2019.

'Software Robots Are Taking Over Many Manual Processes.' *The Times of India*, New Delhi. 9 July 2019.

'Tech Cos Profit from Cloud Biz.' *The Asian Age*, New Delhi. 17 February 2020.

'TIME Names Bono, Bill and Melinda Gates Persons of Year.' *CNN*, www.cnn.com/2005/US/12/18/time.poy/index.html. Accessed on 25 December 2020.

'War of the Words.' *InfoWorld*, 7 February 1994.

'What Is Microsoft Azure Cloud & What Is It Used for?' *Datamation*, www.datamation.com/cloud/microsoft-azure-cloud/. Accessed on 10 December 2020.

'What Is the Bill and Melinda Gates Foundation?' *The Guardian*, 16 March 2015, www.theguardian.com/environment/2015/mar/16/what-is-the-bill-and-melinda-gates-foundation. Accessed on 23 November 2020.

'Why AI Makes a Good Servant, Not Master.' *The Times of India*, New Delhi. 31 March 2019.

Armstrong, Alastair. *The European Reformation: 1500–1610*. Heinemann, 2009.

Cincotta, Howard, editor. *An Outline of American History*. United States Information Agency, 1997.

Eassa, Ashraf. 'Here's How Microsoft Makes Its Money.' *The Motley Fool*, 20 February 2019, www.fool.com/investing/2019/02/19/heres-how-microsoft-makes-its-money.aspx. Accessed on 7 January 2021.

Gates, Bill. 'A Teacher Who Changed My Life.' *Gatesnotes.com*, www.gatesnotes.com/Education/A-Teacher-Who-Changed-My-Life?WT.tsrc=BGFB&linkId=27802897. Accessed on 25 September 2020.

Gates, Bill. 'What I Loved about Paul Allen.' *Gatesnotes.com*, www.gatesnotes.com/About-Bill-Gates/Remembering-Paul-Allen. Accessed on 28 January 2021.

Hartmans, Avery. 'A History of the 30-Year Feud between Bill Gates and Steve Jobs, Whose Love–Hate Relationship Spurred the Success of Microsoft and Apple.' *Business Insider*, www.businessinsider.com/the-bill-gates-steve-jobs-feud-frenemies-2016-3. Accessed on 22 December 2020.

Kapoor, Arushi. 'Even Bill Gates Thinks He Made a Mistake By Not Taking a Holiday in His 20s. Boss, You Listening?' *ScoopWhoop*, 24 June 2019, www.scoopwhoop.com/news/ bill-gates-says-take-a-break/. Accessed on 4 December 2020.

Mejia, Zameena. 'How Steve Ballmer Went from Making $50,000 a Year as an Assistant at Microsoft to Becoming a Billionaire.' *CNBC*, 16 October 2018, www.cnbc. com/2018/07/27/billionaire-steve-ballmer-started-out-making-only-50000-at-microsoft.html. Accessed on 17 December 2020.

Pesce, Nicole Lyn. 'Melinda Gates: Being Married to Bill Gates Is "Incredibly Hard" Sometimes.' *MarketWatch*, 23 April 2019, www.marketwatch.com/story/melinda-gates-being-married-to-bill-gates-is-incredibly-hard-sometimes-2019-04-23/. Accessed on 28 January 2021.

Segal, Troy. 'Who Are Microsoft's (MSFT) Main Competitors?' *Investopedia*, 28 August 2020, www.investopedia.com/ ask/answers/120314/who-are-microsofts-msft-main-competitors.asp. Accessed on 3 January 2021.

Stiffler, Lisa. 'Bill Gates Sr. at 90: A Giant Impact on Technology, Philanthropy and the Seattle Region.' *GeekWire*, 16 September 2020, www.geekwire.com/2015/life-and-times-of-bill-gates-sr-a-giant-impact-on-technology-philanthropy-and-the-seattle-region/. Accessed on 18 December 2020.